Letters from
HMS BRITANNIA

WILLIAM LAMBERT
& THE LATE VICTORIAN NAVY

Letters from HMS BRITANNIA

WILLIAM LAMBERT & THE LATE VICTORIAN NAVY

EDITED BY A. B. DEMAUS

AMBERLEY

O Eternal Lord God, who alone spreadest out the heavens, and rulest the raging of the sea; who hast compassed the waters with bounds until day and night come to an end; Be pleased to receive into thy Almighty and most gracious protection the persons of us thy servants, and the Fleet in which we serve. Preserve us from the dangers of the sea, and from the violence of the enemy; that we may be a safeguard unto our most gracious Sovereign Lady, Queen Victoria, and her Dominions, and a security for such as pass on the seas upon their lawful occasions; that the inhabitants of our island may in peace and quietness serve thee our God; and that we may return in safety to enjoy the blessings of the land with the fruits of our labours, and with a thankful remembrance of thy mercies to praise and glorify thy holy Name; through Jesus Christ our Lord. Amen.

—'Prayer for the Royal Navy' from the *Book of Common Prayer*

First published 2003 by St Leonards Press
as *Upon Their Lawful Occasions*

Amberley Publishing
Cirencester Road, Chalford,
Stroud, Gloucestershire GL6 8PE

www.amberleybooks.com

Copyright © A. B. Demaus 2011

The right of A. B. Demaus to be identified as the Author
of this work has been asserted in accordance with the
Copyrights, Designs and Patents Act 1988.

British Library Cataloguing in Publication Data.
A catalogue record for this book is available from the British Library.

ISBN 978-1-84868-305-1

Typeset in 10pt on 12pt Sabon.
Typesetting and Origination by Amberley Publishing.
Printed in the UK.

Contents

1. W. S. L. on the world voyage in *Wanderer RYS*, 1880–82.

The Lambert Family

Charles Joseph Lambert (1836–88) $\overset{M}{=}$ Susan Bath (1829–98)

—— Catherine Susan Lambert $\overset{M}{=}$ Lt W. R. Clutterbuck, RN
(27/3/1849–16/3/1915)

—— Charles L. Lambert
(1851–20/11/1874)

—— Janet Spears Lambert $\overset{M}{=}$ Henry Black
(1852–?)   one son, two daughters

—— Henry Bath Lambert
(1853–92)

—— Margaret Lambert
(1856–92)

—— Robert Spears Lambert
(1858–1902)

—— Helen M. Lambert $\overset{M}{=}$ (i) Walter Levett (ii) Geoffrey Morgan

—— Beatrice Kate Lambert $\overset{M}{=}$ (i) Hugh Thursby (ii) Clavel Langley

—— George Maximiano Lambert
(1868–91)

—— **William Stanley Lambert $\overset{M}{=}$ Winnifred Hardy**
(1869–1907)

W. S. Lambert –
Navy List Appointments

1 January 1885
Appointed to HMS *Triumph*

15 February 1885
Promoted midshipman

26 February 1889
Promoted acting sub-lieutenant
Appointed to the Royal Naval College, Greenwich

20 December 1890
Sub-lieutenants' examination
Class of certificate:

Seamanship	Navigation	Torpedo	Gunnery	Pilotage
2	3	–	3	2

Promotion to sub-lieutenant backdated to 26 February 1889

20 March 1891
Appointed to HMS *Castor*, RNR drill ship, North Shields
Requalifies in gunnery, HMS *Excellent*

17 April 1891
Appointed HMS *Orlando*, Flag Ship Australia

1 April 1892
Promoted lieutenant

17 November 1892
Appointed to HMS *Mercury*, China Station

18 December 1895
Mercury ordered home

18 June 1896
Short Course, torpedo and gunnery

18 August 1896
Appointed lieutenant in command of HMS *Boxer* (TBD), Mediterranean Station

20 January 1898
Appointed HMS *Barfleur*, China Station (lent from Mediterranean Station)

23 February 1899
Appointed HMS *Duke of Wellington*, Portsmouth Depot

18 March 1900
Last entry on Navy List

Introduction

William Stanley Lambert entered the Royal Navy in 1883 as a cadet, and underwent training on HMS Britannia.[1] The period of his naval career spanned a time of immense and highly significant change in the Senior Service. The Royal Navy, with all the extensive commitments of guarding the interests of Great Britain over a far-flung empire, had already undergone the changes brought about by the transition from sail to steam, but the thinking in the higher echelons of the service was still strongly divided over matters of naval strategy and tactics. Many diehards were still firmly wedded to the priorities of 'spit and polish' – the immaculate turnout of ships and ships' companies, and the performance of routine drills.

To complicate the picture still further, technical development in the last quarter of the nineteenth century was so rapid as to render ships obsolete almost as soon as they were built. An example of the difficulties facing a junior officers in becoming au fait with the rapid technical development at this time may be seen in a remark made by Lambert in his letter dated 1 January 1896, in which he writes, as he was homeward bound from the Far East and expecting a new appointment on his return from leave: 'My present idea is to try for a short course in Gunnery & Torpedo after my leave is up, chiefly for the Gunnery as I have never been shipmates with quickfiring guns & shall be awfully out of it if I went to a modern ship next.'

Outstanding for his far-sightedness and remorseless spirit of reform in this period was Admiral 'Jacky' Fisher, who, relentlessly, and often against opposition and the drag of apathy in high places, forced through practical reforms that reshaped the Navy's thinking and brought the service to a state of efficiency and preparedness by the time the German naval menace (which he had long foreseen) burst onto the world stage in 1914. The long period free from major wars that had elapsed since the heroic days of Nelson and Trafalgar had allowed a false sense of complacency to pervade much of the service. Promotion was slow and junior officers had little opportunity to show initiative. Lambert writes in his letter of 17 July 1896, 'I suppose you noticed that poor old Dan Laxton has got his promotion at last. I am afraid it won't do him much good as he is seventeen and a half years a Lieutenant.'

For these reasons the period 1880–1900 has tended to be rather neglected in the public's knowledge of and appetite for naval affairs. Outside interest in the service is always concentrated on the periods of active service and the 'glamour' of 'war against the enemy'. The surviving letters of W. S. Lambert, covering, with breaks, the whole of his naval career from entry as a cadet to the command of one of the earliest destroyers on active service against the Greeks in Cretan waters in 1897, give an intensely personal view of life in the service at that time. Many of the comments might indeed have been made by any officer of equivalent rank at any time up to and including the Second World War. So, too, does his splendidly dry sense of humour reflect an attribute without which life in the services, in particular in small ships, can be burdensome. Despite the 'growls' about this and that, which are the norm among the members of any of the fighting services, Lambert's deep love of the sea and of the Royal Navy always shows through. He had the enormous advantage of having spent his early boyhood in a seafaring atmosphere, and, indeed, of having sailed round the world in his father's private steam yacht *Wanderer RYS* even before he joined HMS *Britannia*.[2] In some respects he could almost have been considered an old hand before he put on his uniform. *Wanderer RYS* was, at the time she was built in 1878, one of the largest and finest private steam yachts in existence. A composite auxiliary schooner, square-rigged on the fore, she carried 18,000 square feet of sail and was of 708 tons (Thames Measurement). Her trip round the world in 1880–82, with W. S. Lambert aboard, included a passage around the Horn and covered 44,890 miles, of which 13,875 were under sail alone. In his letter home from HMS *Britannia*, dated 14 July 1884, he wrote, 'I am looking forward to being in the *Wanderer* awfully eagerly. I hope some of the new bluejackets will try to make me pay my footing aloft, it will be such a sell for them to know that I have been aloft already in her.'

Lambert retired before reaching the upper ranks, and with his wife Winnifred (née Hardy), he led a comfortable life as a country gentleman of independent means. He came from a large family that had always had many friends in England and elsewhere. Most of Lambert's service had been overseas, so his retirement enabled him and Winnifred to renew those relationships at leisure. Sadly, his protracted foreign service had left its legacy on his health and he died in 1907 at the early age of thirty-eight, having enjoyed his retirement for only seven years.

10 February–14 December 1884
Letters from HMS *Britannia*

Thanks very much for your letter which I received this morning. I found out yesterday that Kirke, one of my term, knows a chap at Forsters called de Kantlow who has a sister called Sophy. This is the girl Beatrice was humbugging Edgar about when he was at Park Lane last holidays. Please ask the girls if they write to him not to mention this as I am going to have a joke with him. Kirke, if possible, is going to get a photo of her, which I will send to him. I got a mod yesterday from Brunel, the French master. But it was not at all my fault. Brunel told us all not to talk or he would give us a mod. Then he thought he saw me speak and said, 'Lambert, mod!' I at once said, 'Please sir, I did not say a word.' Then he said, 'Well, you have now,' and gave me a mod. I was going to Aldous the Principal Naval Instructor to try and get let off only there was not time before I had to drill it, and after that it was not worth while. I enclose a photo of Halsey which I got a day or two ago. I think it is rather a good one, do not you?

We have been having several football matches lately. The last two were Port *v.* Starboard and 3rd Term *v.* 2nd Term. Both of them were drawn. … There is a concert coming off soon, at least at the end of term. The athletic sports come off on the 19th of March … Could you send me a Cricketers' Companion for 1884? I promised to get one for Kirke. They are one shilling each and are to be got at the following address:

James Lillywhite, Cricket Warehouse, 10 Symons St, Euston Square, London NW.

I am also rather short of stamps now. Could you send me some? There is a paper being got up in the ship now to which the cadets send articles. It costs 3*d* a week to defray printing expenses. It comes out monthly and I am going to get one every month. If you would like me to send it on to you when I get it please write and say so. I think I have expended all my news so I will stop.

Believe me, your affectionate son,

W. S. Lambert

I send you the first number of the *Britannia*.[3] Will you please keep it for me as I want to keep them all and have them bound or something when I leave the ship … We have

Feb⁷ 10ᵗʰ 1884

My dear Mother

Thanks very much for your letter which I rec⁴ this morning. I found out yesterday that Kirke, one of term iso knows & a chap at Forsters called de Kantzow who has a sister called Sophy. This is the girl Beatrice was humbugging Edgar about when he was ~~here~~ at ~ . dane last holidays. Please ask

2. The opening page of the first of the quoted letters of W. S. L., dated 10 February 1884.

3. HMS *Britannia* and *Hindostan* moored in the Dart estuary before the building of the Britannia Royal Naval College on shore.

been having a lot of Football lately, but all that is in the *Britannia*. 'Observer' is my instructor and is an awfully fine chap and a great sportsman. What a joke this Bill of Censure is. I hope the Commons pass it and old Gladstone is kicked out. I am seeing this term how little I can spend at the stores etc. this term. I think the 'Battle of Port Said' is awfully amusing. Have you read it? I was nearly put on deck this afternoon for making a row on the sleeping deck only I proved to them that I was not in the sleeping deck at the time they mentioned. (Sold again!!!) Coles was put on deck for fagging this afternoon for which he will probably get a caning. This will take away his conduct for the term and as he was warned last term on account of his bad conduct, he will probably get turned out of the ship at the end of the term. On this account he went up to Lieut. Thomas who had ordered him to be sent before the Commander tomorrow, and asked to be let off as it was his last chance but Thomas refused which was rather beastly of him, I think. I must put a stop to this rot so with love to all,

 I remain,
  Your affectte [*sic*] son,
   W. S. Lambert

P.S. Braithwaite has told all our class that they had better get bow compasses (for ink only) for making figures of Euclid. They are about so long and something like the above drawing but not much. W. S. L.

24/2/1884

Thanks awfully for the compasses which I received on Thursday. I am very sorry I did not write before but I have had such an awful lot of work to do that Sunday is almost the only day I can write on … We had a football match on Friday, Brunel's classes *v.* Houssaye's classes (the two French instructors). … Sad to relate I will not be able to obtain Sophy de K's photo for Edgar. Could you send me some newspaper wrappers (only two or three) to wrap the *Britannia* in when it comes out … There is nothing more to say so I will stop, with love to all,

 I remain,
  Your loving son,
   W. S. Lambert

P.S. Please send me some etching pens as we have to put land into our charts now and other pens are too thick.

2/3/1884

Thanks awfully for the etching pens and book. I am sorry I did not write sooner but I did not have time. The third term is always the hardest working term there is such a lot to do. The concert came off last Tuesday and was very good. I enclose the programme. About the jolliest thing was 'Sir Bevill' by Mrs Bainbridge, the Commander's wife. 'Political Economy', a reading by the English master, was awfully good too. It was taken from Mark Twain's or Bret Harte or some other Yankee. Captain Smith recited the Inchcape Rock awfully well. The Glee Club was decent too with Cadets for high voices and Login, the Captain, the English master, and Mr Aldous for basses. We have had one or two football matches late[ly], Odd Classes *v.* Even Classes was drawn with 3 goals each and our term beat the 2nd term by 3 goals.

𝕳.𝕸.𝕾.　　Britannia.

TUESDAY, FEBRUARY 26, 1884.

OVERTURE	*Crown Diamonds. Auber.*	The Band.
GLEE	*Since first I saw your face*	The Glee Club.
RECITATION	*The Inchcape Bell.*	Capt. Bowden Smith
GLEE	*Let the hills resound with song*	The Glee Club.
SONG	*'Sir Bevill'*	Mrs. Bainbridge.
HORNPIPE	Messrs. Grenfell, Shelford, Fair, Grant, Hamilton & Jeffreys
SELECTION	*Rigoletto. Verdi.*	The Band
READING	*'Political Economy'*	Mr. Hamilton Williams
DUET	*I would that my love, Mendelssohn.*	Mrs. Bowden Smith and Mrs. Bainbridge
GLEE	*O hush thee, my Babie*	The Glee Club.
QUARTETTE	*'Iolanthe'*	Messrs Hickley and Macaulay, *Violins* Mr. Luce, *Violoncello.* Mr. Brock, *Piano*
IRISH JIG		Messrs. Grenfell, Shelford, Grant and Jeffreys
GLEE	*Ye Mariners of England!*	The Glee Club.

GOD SAVE THE QUEEN.

4. Programme of concert given on HMS *Britannia* on 26 February 1884.

9/3/1884

Thanks awfully for the paper and the letter. I am surprised at the girls running away from a 'pig'. Indeed, I am more shocked than surprised. They should have formed a square and met the enemy at the point of the umbrella. Could you let me go on leave with Halsey to a Mrs Schuster who lives at Torquay? We have had lovely weather lately. Regular summer's days. I have been playing football a good deal lately. I think it is an awful fine game

March 11th. ... I had to stop on Sunday and have not had time to continue till now. Could you send me a good lot of stamps, say about two or three bobs' worth, as I want to get a model masthead lantern from some shop whose address a chap knows. I promised to get one for one of the seamanship instructors called Stevens. He wants one to fix up a model he has. There is no more time so I must stop.

P.S. Please send leave (if I may go) as soon as possible, as I want to go next Saturday.

23/3/1884

I am beastly sorry I did not write before but I really seem to have hardly any time whatever to myself. A few days ago the funeral of Le Comte de la Houssaye took place. He was one of the French masters. Any cadets who liked might go to the funeral so I thought I should like to go. He used to know Bob at Storrington. We went down to Dartmouth in a pinnace, about 80 of us, and marched to the church where his body was. Then we marched after the hearse to the cemetery (distant about 2 miles) in a most blazing sun. It was awfully hot. He was buried by two Roman Catholic priests and after the ceremony we went back to the cricket field. I enjoyed myself awfully at Mrs Schuster's; she is awfully nice and kind. She is a German. When we came away she invited us to an assault-at-arms which took place on the next Wednesday. We went of course and it was awfully fine. Our two gymnasium sergeants performed on the horizontal bar. On Friday last we played Apsley House (a school at Torquay). We won by 10 goals to nothing.

I regret to state that I lost all those stamps you sent me the same morning. I think I must have dropped them under the breakfast table and then the messroom servants would bag them like a shot. I have since discovered that the model lights cost 9*d* or post free 1*s* so could you send me 1/- worth. I am awfully sorry to have bothered you so. There is going to be a concert tomorrow, the chief event of which is a Toy Symphony. Also a Blue-jacket will dance a hornpipe. I will write and tell you about it soon if I have time.

With love to all,
  I remain,
    Your loving son,
      W. S. Lambert

N.B. When will Father and Bob arrive?

30/3/1884

It seems an awfully short time now before we come home for the holidays. I write now to ask if when we come home, Halsey could come to lunch with us, arriving as we do at about 2 o'clock, he would be so beastly late for lunch. Mr Thomas, the Lieutenant whom you saw when you came down, has been appointed Lieut.-Commander of the *Wave* vice Mr Login. It is an awfully good step for him as he has not got eight years seniority as Lieut. yet. But the worst of it is that Mr Login will have to go, so I will have no cabin to resort to as I have now. I am at present writing in his cabin. I hope some jolly Lieut. will come here instead of Thomas. It would be a joke if he was one we know.

Yesterday we had a paperchase which was an awful joke but unfortunately we could not catch the hares. Next Wednesday the Sports come off but I am not in for anything because I am so awfully out of condition. How jolly it will be having Father and Bob back again. It seems ages since they were here (I mean to say in England.) The racquet tournament came off a few days ago and was won by a fourth term cadet captain called Johnson. There is no more to say therefore I will stop.

25/4/1884

I had no time to write anything last night except that scribble I sent you. I got here all right and the train was punctual. You cannot imagine how awfully uncomfortable everything feels here after home; the hammocks, the food, etc. I was so awfully sorry to leave you yesterday but there are only twelve or thirteen weeks before I hope to see the *Wanderer* come into the harbour. ...

4/5/1884

Thanks awfully for the leave to go to Mrs Shuster etc. whenever I like. It will save a lot of trouble. A few days ago I got a letter from Login. He is on the *Vernon* going through a short course of Torpedo and Gunnery.[4] The *Wave* has been finished now and goes out twice a week but only the 4th Term go out in her so I have not been in her while under weigh yet but only to drill at the sails etc. She is much jollier than the *Dapper* in every way.[5] ... It is raining like anything now and has been with intervals for the past week or ten days. I suppose that Papa and Bob are down at Cowes now. I wish you would send me a pair of brushes (without handles) as of my two brushes one has disappeared and the other is coming to pieces. Also I should like a box of Ludie's pens (medium point). I am playing cricket a good deal now (that is practising at nets) and am also playing tennis. The paper (*Britannia*) is coming out on next Saturday. We were to have played the Channel Fleet at cricket yesterday only they have not arrived in Plymouth yet.

There is no time for more and no more to say if there was time so I will stop.

I am,
  Your loving son,
  W. S. Lambert

N.B. Halsey has come back.

11/5/1884

I am sorry I have not written for some time. I have probably mentioned Hall to you, well, he has got 14 days second class for fagging a new. Second Class is the worst punishment you can get, and 14 days is the most you can get at a time. He nearly got reported to the Admiralty when he would have been dismissed [from] the ship. Also Reeves, the chap I collect stamps for, got a study report for reading a novel at Physics. (He was reported by Von Tunzelman.) He was originally chief captain of cadets but is now reduced to the ranks so to speak. A chap called Grenfell was made captain in his place. He is a cousin of Captain Grenfell who was in the *Cockatrice* at Constantinople.[6] I enclose a photo of Lieut. Stokes for you to put in my book. Tell

Nellie that the photo of the *Wave* will arrive soon. I went yesterday to Mrs Schuster on leave and we had a very jolly time. It has been very hot for the last two days, regular summer's days. Thanks awfully for the brushes; they are awfully jolly. No time for more.

18/5/1884

Thanks awfully for your letter which I received yesterday … On Wednesday last we played the 82nd Regiment at cricket and got licked. Yesterday (Saturday) we played the Engineer College of Plymouth and won by 27 runs.

Talking of cricket, may I have a bat from our professional, Underwool. I have to get leave from home as several cases are known when Cadets have got bats against their parent's will. It will be charged in the bill. Can you tell me Dr Gray's address as I want to write to him. I am so glad the old *Wanderer* is fitting out. Will we be at Cowes during the Regetta, do you know? It is awfully fine weather here now and has been for the last week or so. The country is awfully pretty here now, the may is out and there are a lot of yellow irises growing by the banks of the streams. My servant McCarlthy has been superannuated and I have got a chap called Taylor instead. I think he is a much better servant than McCarlthy. There is simply nothing to say so I will stop.

I am

Your affectionate son,

W. S. Lambert

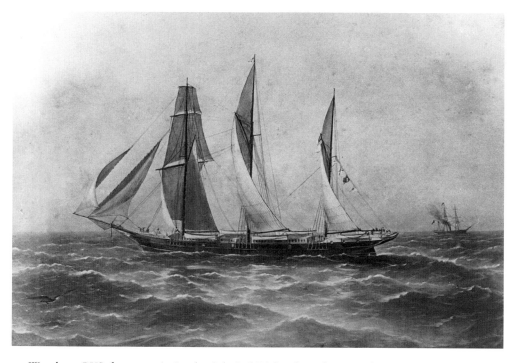

5. *Wanderer RYS*, from a painting by Admiral Richard Brydges Beechey (1808–95). This dates from 1879, before the vessel was refitted with additional accommodation fore and aft.

6. *A Voyage round the World*, a painting by P. H. Calderon, RA. It shows Mrs Lambert and the four children (W. S. L. third from left) in the *Wanderer*'s saloon, 1879.

8/6/1884

Thanks very much for your letter which I got this morning. I enclose the letters of Share and Dr Gray. I have got the former at last after about a year's waiting. I wish you would send me a *Cricketer's Companion* price 1s 2d from J. Lillywhite's Cricketing Warehouse, 10 Seymour Street, Euston Square. I want it for Marowbery because he takes a great interest in cricket and did not know how to get one. We have had two matches since last I wrote, one against the Marines which we won & the other against South Devon which we lost. Several chaps have got chicken-pox now but none are at all bad …

I went out in one of the sailing cutters belonging to the ship this afternoon. There was an awfully jolly breeze and we were several times gunwale under. Bathing has begun now but the water is still very cold. In the *Britannia* I sent you the 'The Dream of Olden Days' was written by the English master, Hamilton Williams; the 'Cadet's first day on a sea-going Ship' by Captn Bowden-Smith, the puzzle by Willis of my term and the cricketing news by Collins of my term. There is a mistake in the printing at the top of the last page. It puts Vivian 6; Trotman o; Collins 6; Trotman 6. It means Vivian b (bowled) Trotman &c.

I must stop now.

With love to you all,

I am,

Your loving son,

W. S. Lambert

P.S. Can you send me some newspaper wrappers for *Britannia*? Will you send foreign paper, photo and stamps as I want to write to Share soon.

7. W. S. L. (extreme left) at a tennis party at Ringlee, Queenstown, when a naval cadet, *c.* 1884.

15/6/1884

Thanks awfully for the newspaper wrappers which I have just received. I hope to goodness you will come round here in the *Wanderer*. Captain Bowden-Smith told me that he had got a letter from Admiral Cator saying something about her coming round. Is the latter going with you for the cruises? I played cricket yesterday for the first time & made 6 not out; awfully swell, was not it? I am going to write and tell Max because he told me that when he played last he made o. Yesterday we played the Naval Team and who should appear on the XI but Mr Le Marchant. He did not recognise me but I went up and spoke to him. He said that he had seen you in town a few days ago but he had no idea I was here. We licked them easily by about 50 runs in the first innings. There was no time for the second innings. The weather here is awfully jolly but it is fearfully hot work playing cricket. I hope the Health Exhibition will be on when I go to London next I should think it must be very jolly. I must stop now or there will not be time to write to Max.

  I remain,
    Your affectionate son,
      W. S. Lambert

1/7/1884

I hope you are quite well as I have not heard from you for about a week. Bob and Harry came on Saturday evening, late, so I did not see them till 1 o'clock on Sunday. I stayed on board in the afternoon till 9 o'clock when I came back. I think the *Snowdrop* is an awfully jolly little yawl and most awfully roomy. Tell Nellie Bob has a mania for adding the word 'drop' to everything he says. For instance, if you say, 'Would you like some strawberries?' he calmly remarks, 'Strawberry drop.' He also calls everything shipshape. Yesterday the Channel Fleet came in to Torbay and a lot of mids came into Dartmouth to see the ship, amongst others Tom Morgan and Farquhar. The latter was in the *Iron Duke* when we were at Hong Kong.⁷ Will you send me my copy of the *Wanderer* book, I think it is in the chest of drawers in my room. Such a lot of chaps want to know what she is like and all about her that I think I had better have it to refer to. By the bye, can you send me a Bradshaw? I always like having one at the end of the term in case of emergencies.

14/7/1884

I write now to tell you that I am going to alter my usual train as I have discovered my last choice gets to London quicker than the usual one. I am coming (if you consent) by the 7.13 train, which gets to Vauxhall at 2.23. Will you write at once to O'Neill, the Paymaster (I do not know how to spell his name) and tell him to take my ticket for Exeter and give me £2 journey money for my ticket to Waterloo etc. That is the amount most chaps get who go the same way. Today our exams began. Our day's exam was Drawing. We began by a diagram which took an hour and a half. We then had to do the model of a boatshed with a boat in it. It was awfully difficult for, as you know, drawing is not my strong point. This afternoon the examination for gymnasium prizes came off. The places and marks are as follows:

Johnson (a)	181 marks	Ship's prize
Silver	177 "	4th term
Hamilton	142 "	3rd "
Carvick	160 "	2nd "
Armstrong	151 "	1st "

The swimming races come off on Saturday. They are to be swum in flannel trousers and shirts. I think I shall go in for my term race but I expect I shall be somewhere at the wrong end at the finish. When are you going to join the *Wanderer*? I am looking forward to being in the *Wanderer* awfully eagerly. I hope some of the new bluejackets will try to make me pay my footing aloft, it will be such a sell for them to know that I have been aloft already in her. I must stop now for want of something to say.

23/8/1884
Somewhere between Edinburgh and Stafford

Dear Max,
  We had a very jolly drive to Kingussie but the coach was crammed to overflowing. One man sat on the luggage right on top. The last few stages we galloped nearly all the time, all the mail bags on the road at small places being chucked up as we passed. At Kingussie there was not a single first-class seat in the train so we had to go second class and even then we could hardly get three seats in one compartment. At Perth we changed and got into a 1st class carriage and went most of the way to

Edinburgh alone. At Stirling we ran over a large mastiff. It ran along right under the train for some time without being touched but then it tried to get away under, and its head was run over. At the hotel, Edinburgh, I found an acquaintance in the shape of a midshipman called Clarke who passed out last term with eleven months sea time so that now he has become a mid without having to pass an exam. He is now travelling with us and is going to London. We get to Stafford at about half past five. Tell Beatrice I hope her fleshlings will arrive. We told the shopgirl to send them to her as they did not get to the shop till eleven and our train started at ten. Did you have good sport on Friday and has the *Saucy* arrived?[8]

Your loving brother,
W. S. Lambert

26/9/1884

I have not much time to write as I have got to work. Dr Gray sent me the enclosed prescription to take. The doctor here, not having the ingredients, told me to send it home to be made up. Will you please send me a bottle and keep the prescription as perhaps I may want another bottle. I will get my photo taken as soon as I can. Bathing will stop tomorrow as the water is getting beastly cold. I must stop now and work. I will write again soon.

I am,
Your affectionate son,
W. S. Lambert

8/10/1884

I want you to send me a Postal Order for £1 as I have bought a Stamp book from a chap as I am going to collect stamps. Please send it as soon as possible as he is in rather a hurry for it. We have begun winter routine now but it is still quite hot and we are nearly roasted as we have to wear our thickest clothes whether we like it or not. It has been a beastly wet day today but we managed to play a little cricket in the odd free moments.

If you are in want of a birthday present to give me you can get me a stamp book price 13/6 called *The Imperial*. It is in two volumes and is to be got at Stanley Gibbons & Co., 8 Gower Street, London WC. I must stop now and work.

13/11/1884

Thanks awfully for the stamps etc. I am all right now, thank goodness, and very glad to get to work again. My instructor says that the interval in my work will do me more good than harm so you need not trouble about that. I suppose you have seen my photos by this time? Aren't they awful? Please write to say where I am to send them. To London, I suppose. I must stop and go to Seamanship Class …

24/11/1884

On Saturday last we had our Essay exam. I got through my Essay pretty well but some chaps only did about a page of theirs. In the afternoon I went on leave to Mr Von Tunzelmann. He has a pupil for Sandhurst who is an awfully jolly chap. We went out for a walk along the cliffs and had an awful spree. Oh! will you send me some etching pens for the exams. I have just spoilt the last one I had and they are almost indispensable for charts. The end of the term seems to be getting awfully close now, does it not? Will the house be full at Christmas as if not I should like Halsey to stay for a day or two directly after we come home just as he did before. I must stop now ...

30/11/1884

I enclose two of each sort of my photo and also Nellie's letter to Max. Last night we had a ventriloquist and conjuror down here. He was rather good. The ventriloquist part was with two figures who talk to one another and sing etc. What do you think I had better do? Get my plain clothes when my outfitter comes down here? Or wait till the holidays and get them with Max's help? I should think the latter would be the best as I never know what patterns to choose. By the bye, when do Max's holidays begin?

1/12. Yesterday afternoon I went to lunch and dinner with Captain Bainbridge, the commander. He said that he had received a letter from Captain Rose saying that he wanted four or five boys for the *Triumph* if the Commander could get some to put down their names for it.[9] The Commander said that he had talked to Captain Bowden-Smith about it and they both thought that it was a very good place to go and they have a good instructor on the flagship. The Commander told me to write home and tell you about this as if you and Papa consented, he would put down my name for it. I asked him who the Commander was and he said Captain Simpson. He is the chap who went up to Kioto with us. Could you send me £3. I feel awfully ashamed of writing for so much but I will really want it as I have to tip all sorts of people, servant, his assistant, seamanship instructor, mess-room servant and several others. If you will send it please send it in Postal Orders, not a Post Office order as anybody can change a Postal Order but a Post Office Order I would have to change myself and 10 to 1 I could not get leave into Dartmouth to change it. We are going to have theatricals at the end of this term only cadets do not act as they would not have time to learn their parts and do their work at the same time. I wish that the *Britannia* was not so far from London because it is rather a joke seeing the prizes given away. I am afraid I will not get any but I might get the seamanship prize. I hope so, I am sure. Tell Katie she will have to work me up in dancing these holidays as I have promised to go to Halsey's party. Fancy me coming out in the dancing line, going to parties etc.! I am coming home as usual by the 2.40 train getting to London about 9. The day is the 18th. I will be heartily glad to get out of the ship. Everything gets so monotonous going on exactly the same routine for two years. I must stop now and write to Max.

• • •

From the journal of HMS *Britannia*, April 1885:

HMS Triumph, St Vincent
From a correspondent

We started from Plymouth on Saturday, the 7th of February, which, of course, you know already. It was blowing a little but not very much, and soon most of the fellows began to feel a little bit queer.

Sunday, the 8th, it was blowing a little fresher, everyone turned out of his hammock, but all feeling a little, and some very, squeamish. We set our jib, a three-cornered sail, but no sooner was the jib hoisted than the jibboom, a rather light spar, snapped clean off, carrying a man who was on it away into the sea. The life-boat was away in less than a minute, and he was picked up. He received rather a bad knock over the eye from a splinter, or something of that sort.

We lay to all day getting in the wreck of the jibboom, and did not start ahead again until the evening, when the wind was not blowing so hard, and the sea had gone down a bit. Everyone of us were [*sic*] ill now except Lambert and myself (that is to say, of our term). I did not feel perfectly right, but I could keep watch and walk about and eat, and I had a very fair share of watch-keeping too; as Hamilton and. Pasley, who are in my watch, both turned in about mid-day on Sunday, and did not turn out till Tuesday morning. The gun-room was now afloat with water coming through every port and hole in the ship's side, and we in consequence had to live outside it with a screen up. Monday the 9th, the wind had abated, but there was still some sea on. None of the Cadets who were ill turned out.

Tuesday, the 10th, everyone turned out, though they were not all well. Nothing now happened until the 12th, when we set all plain sail and hoisted our screw out of the water, and sailed until the evening of Friday the 13th, when we shortened sail to topsails: that is, we took in top gallant sails and royals, and lowered our screw and steamed slowly.

Nothing happened on Saturday the 14th.

Sunday, the 15th, we had Church in the main battery; and after Church those Naval Cadets who had eleven months [seniority] were promoted to the rank of Midshipman.

Of course we had now settled down in the gunroom again, and all our 'goods and chattels' had been stowed away under the table.

Monday, the 16th, was a fine day with nice sunshine. It was my first watch from 8–12 (at night that is), but as there are three of us in a watch, two of us keep two hours a piece, and the third gets a night in. Well, it was my second part of the watch, and I turned in at 8 p.m., with my clothes on ready to be out smartly at ten o'clock, the night being very fine and starlight, with a gentle breeze. At ten o'clock I was roused out by the Mid. of the first part of the watch to hear, through a ventilator which is close to my hammock, a tremendous row on deck, and learnt from the Mid. that it was blowing a middle-aged hurricane.

I put on my sea-boots, my waterproof and my sou'wester and went on deck. The ropes were blowing against one another and the canvas mast covers (which are put on the mast to keep the blacks from the funnel making the mast dirty) were blowing about all over the place, and in fact you couldn't imagine such a noise without being there. The force of the wind increased every minute until about half-past eleven it was blowing a hurricane, at least it was so logged. There was a continual fall of spray on the decks and I was very glad to be well prepared for it. It was a circular gale which goes by the name of a hurricane or cyclone in different parts of the world, and you get the wind first on one side of the vessel and then on the other side. I had to hold on very tightly to anything I could get hold of when I was walking about, as sea-boots are fearfully slippery things on wet decks, and when once they begin to slip all you can do is to bend forward and catch hold of the first thing you can as you pass it, putting your hands out in front of you to prevent breaking your shins against some sharp bit of iron or wood. I turned in at twelve midnight and the next morning it was quite fine.

Tuesday, 17th, nothing happened. I had the second part of the middle watch, that is from 2 a.m. to 4 a.m., and just at the end it began to rain a little and continued until about Wednesday 18th, at noon. It now began to blow a bit right ahead and the sea began to get a little confused. At about four o'clock we were going full speed with a heavy sea, when we made a tremendous plunge into an extra big wave and lost our second jibboom. I enclose an illustration of the accident.

Thursday, 19th. We fitted a spar about 6ft long as a jibboom so as to stay the top-gallant mast. Thursday evening we lit up all the boilers and went ahead as hard as

8. The brigs HMS *Liberty* and HMS *Sealark*, seen in the Dart estuary. They were used as sail-training tenders to HMS *Britannia*.

we could and Friday morning when I turned out we were alongside Porto Santo, the first of the islands, and by 2 o'clock we were anchored off Madeira.

I went ashore at about 3.30 and immediately went for a delightful ride, Mr and Mrs B—— being out. We went to the top of Telegraph Hill, which I have no doubt you remember, from which we got a very extensive view. We then rode to a relation's house, and after dinner we played cards and had a very nice evening. This morning I returned on board at eight o'clock, and have just received home letters.

You say that you think it impossible that I escaped sea-sickness, but I did, as you see by the commencement of this letter. It is very different to crossing the channel in a mail packet, and there is always plenty to do here. The ship behaves very well in a gale for we certainly had it with very full measure.

I shall go ashore to-morrow and dine at Quinta. Lambert, I believe the Captain, and a guest he has here, and Lieut. Gibbons are going to dine there. There is such a change from rain and bad weather, a lovely day with hot sun, so delicious.

We started from Madeira, after a very pleasant sojourn there indeed, on Wednesday, February 26th, in lovely weather. We steamed for the remainder of the day, and next day set all sail with studding sails, being now in the trade winds. We then put out our fires and hoisted our screw out of the water.

This is my month for helping the Staff-Commander in navigating the ship, and I began my duties on the first day of the month. It excuses me from all other duties and school.

We sailed on until yesterday, making an average of seven-and-a-half knots, whereas we should have gone only five knots under steam.

We lowered our screw about six o'clock last evening and commencing steaming we furled sails; being now in sight of land, that is. We could see it when the clouds cleared for a minute.

I forgot to say that Monday evening we caught a dolphin, and a very pretty fish he is, wearing a coat of many colours. I had to stay on deck until 1.30 a.m., when we got into a much better anchorage than we had at Madeira, being thoroughly sheltered.

9. The Torpedo Class, Portsmouth, 1880. Seated second left is William R. Clutterbuck (later admiral), W. S. L.'s brother-in-law, who had married his eldest sister Catherine (Kate).

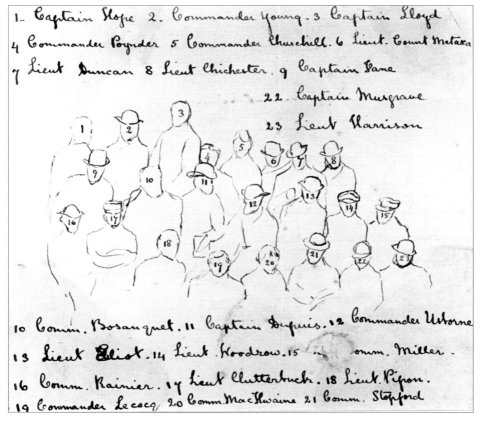

1 Captain Hope 2. Commander Young 3 Captain Lloyd
4 Commander Poynder 5 Commander Churchill. 6 Lieut. Count Metaxa
7 Lieut Duncan 8 Lieut Chichester. 9 Captain Jane
                              22 Captain Musgrave
                              23 Lieut Harrison

10 Comm. Bosanquet. 11 Captain Dupuis. 12 Commander Usborne
13 Lieut Eliot. 14 Lieut Woodrow. 15 ... omm. Miller.
16 Comm. Rainier. 17 Lieut Clutterbuck. 18 Lieut Pipon.
19 Commander Lecocq, 20 Comm. MacIlwaine 21 Comm. Stopford

10. The Torpedo Class, Portsmouth, 1880. Key to the above.

The island of St Vincent looks very barren, but I hear there is some quail shooting, and I and my fellow navigating Mid. Reeves, and the Chief Quarter-Master, who is also of a navigating species, are going ashore to see if we can find any.

We are all turned out of the gun-room again on account of wet; it is a nuisance the way in which this ship has been turned out of the dockyard, every port nearly in the ship leaks.

I am afraid that I have not so much to say about this passage, as we had such a very quiet and smooth one.

We did not go shooting on Wednesday, as we were not allowed to land before 3.30 on account of the heat, but I landed with Reeves and Arent for a walk round the town, which consists of a lot of dirty little low huts, I don't believe there is a two-storey house in the place.

Thursday I landed with Reeves about one o'clock, both with our guns, and started shooting. We came across several hawks, of which I shot one, and Reeves shot another, the first bird I have shot on the wing.

This morning I landed with the Staff-Commander to take sights. I shall land this afternoon to shoot. We start to-morrow for Monte Video.

• • •

14/12/1884

Thanks very much for your last letter which I received this morning. We have finished all our exams now except the seamanship which comes off on the next three days. I expect I shall get eight months sea time. We had an awful joke this morning. A second term youth refused to fag for one of our term so we licked him with a fives bat. This enraged his term who think that as it is so close to the end of term they won't fag for us, so they asked us (our term) to fight them (N.B. Beastly cheek!) so we licked a few of the ringleaders and reduced the remainder to order with sundry kicks, smacks etc. I told you in my last epistle that I should reach Paddington about nine but I expect it will be earlier, about half past eight. How I do pity Bill Clutterbuck at Zanzibar. I have heard that it is a beastly hole and if it is anything half so bad as Dartmouth he must be in a miserable state. It has done nothing but blow and rain etc. for the last fortnight. The whole place is something foul and disgusting. I am rather vicious tonight, you notice, but I feel utterly done up by the exams and I think I should have gone mad if they had gone on much longer. You cannot think how they knock you up. I feel tired all day and night and in this weather you can hardly ever go ashore and get fresh air. I must stop now and go and turn in.

   I remain,
      Your affectionate son,
         W. S. Lambert

25 January 1885–26 August 1887
Letters from HMS *Triumph*

25/1/1885

I was so very sorry to say goodbye to you last Tuesday. I went up and got leave from the Commander next morning and started by the eleven train from Portsmouth ... Next morning I ordered breakfast at 10 but was half an hour late so I had to hurry considerably to get to Queen's Road at 11. Knighton Warren kept me over two hours, I was nearly dead with fatigue when he said that he would stop ... I started for Portsmouth at half past nine next morning and got down about 12, only just having time to shift before going on watch for four hours. In the evening I went to dine with Captain Markham on the *Vernon*. There I found Mr Mure, a Sub who acted as the female in the theatricals we saw when we were at Queenstown ...

Yesterday at about half past one we went out of harbour and tried the engines and now we are anchored at Spithead which is not half so nice as the dockyard being so far out. I am going to try and get up to London tomorrow for a day or so to get some things. I must stop now and write to Nellie.

Ever your loving son,
W. S. Lambert

1/2/1885
Spithead

We did not go on Saturday after all as it was blowing so hard that they could not hoist the steam pinnace and now we have to wait till tomorrow afternoon as we have to change our steam cutter. It is awfully riling as it is beastly out here. It is over half an hour's pull to the shore. I do pity you poor people having to stay in England all in the cold, at least, if you have it half as cold as it is down here. I am going to try and get leave to go to Dartmouth and see the *Britannia* when we are at Plymouth. Have you heard from Bill lately? I suppose he is still being roasted in Zanzibar. However, that is better than being frozen in England. This month I am let off watch, school, boat duty etc. as I have to help the Staff Commander. I went to dinner a few days ago with Captain Markham of the *Vernon* and afterwards went to the circus. The only good thing in it was some boxing between the ex-champion of the world and the Champion of England. The champion of the world had a table

11. Officers of HMS *Triumph*. W. S. L. is seated, front row, seventh from the left.

12. HMS *Triumph* at Malta.

simply crowded with trophies such as silver belts, gold and silver cups, medals etc. I must stop now.

Always remaining,
Your affectionate brother,
W. S. Lambert

13/6/1885

I came on board this morning at 8 o'clock from the hotel and found the gunroom occupants engaged in having breakfast so I joined them. My chest arrived this morning but they have not put in a uniform great coat so I am going to order one tomorrow if I can get leave. This afternoon I went and knocked about this dockyard ... We have not been doing any duty today. I do not know when we begin duty. The ship is in an awful mess now what with getting in stores etc. ...

26/8/1887
11 p.m.
Esquimalt

W. S. Lambert from his hammock dictates to the writer hereof who is closing the mail for the South: – Oh! bother! there is not time to state all the excuses he is inventing for not having enclosed a letter this time – the real truth is pure laziness ...

• • •

HMS *Triumph*, as flagship of Rear-Admiral Sir Michael Culme-Seymour, accompanied HMS *Cormorant* (composite sloop, 1877) to Esquimalt, British Colombia, for the opening of the new dry dock there on 20 July 1887. W. S. L. was present on that occasion. It is unfortunate that no further letters from his time on the *Triumph* survive, apart from the fragment dated 26 August 1887 from Esquimalt.

13. HMS *Triumph* at Esquimalt, Vancouver Island, July 1887, on the occasion of the official opening of the dry dock there.

14. Admiral Sir Michael Culme-Seymour when commander-in-chief, Portsmouth, with his staff.

15. HMS *Triumph* off Cape de Gatte.

W. S. L. was promoted to acting sub-lieutenant on 26 February 1889 and was appointed to the Royal Naval College, Greenwich, for his sub-lieutenant's course. The Royal Naval College, formerly at Portsmouth, was transferred to Greenwich in 1873, where it occupied the old Greenwich Hospital, closed as such in 1869. Here W. S. L. studied for his sub-lieutenants' examination, which he took on 20 December 1890. He was promoted to sub-lieutenant, and was confirmed in this rank with seniority from 26 February 1889, i.e. with seniority back-dated to his appointment as acting sub-lieutenant.

He was then appointed to HMS *Castor*, a Royal Naval Reserve (RNR) drill ship at North Shields. HMS *Castor* was an old fifth-rater of 1832, finally sold out of naval service in 1902. The RNR was formed as a distinct reserve in 1859, at first for ratings only, but in 1861 for Sub-Lieutenants and Lieutenants also. The RNR was organised on a territorial basis, with bases, often old and outdated warships, in major ports around Britain's shores. As a newly qualified Sub-Lieutenant, W. S. L. would have been employed mainly on instructional and parade duties while on HMS *Castor*. He trained RNR ratings, and perhaps junior officers.

W. S. L.'s next appointment, a requalification in gunnery on HMS *Excellent*, dated from 20 March 1891. Thus he would have been among the earliest officers to do so on HMS *Excellent*, since *Excellent* was newly 'commissioned' at Whale Island, Portsmouth, in that year. *Excellent* built up a formidable reputation as the gunnery school of the Royal Navy and became a byword for smartness and efficiency. W. S. L.'s course in *Excellent* was a short one, since he was not a specialist gunnery officer, and three weeks later, on 17 April 1891, having completed his short course, he was appointed to HMS *Orlando*, Flag Ship Australia.[10]

16. HMS *Orlando*. W. S. L. was appointed to her as from 17 April 1891, when she was Flag Ship Australia. (*Imperial War Museum*)

He had not long taken up this appointment in Australia before he was sent to join HMS *Royalist*, at the time off the south-east coast of New Guinea. While still in *Royalist* he wrote from the Union Club, Sydney, with news of his promotion to lieutenant, and also of his surprise at being ordered to return home. By 8 December 1892 we find W. S. L. writing from HMS *Tamar*, a troopship,[11] then eastbound to China, W. S. L. having been appointed from 17 November 1892 to HMS *Mercury* at the China Station.[12] W. S. L.'s letters of 16 January 1893, 18 January 1893 and 1 February 1893 reveal that the *Mercury's* recommissioning was far from smooth. The new arrivals had to be accommodated wherever space could be found for them; at the same time, the *Mercury* was undergoing refit. In W. S. L.'s case, this accommodation was aboard HMS *Wivern*, an old rigged turret ironclad of 1863.[13] Fate intervened again before W. S. L. could settle finally aboard *Mercury*, for by 19 February 1893 we find him in HMS *Caroline*, sent at short notice to replace one of her lieutenants on the sick list.[14] Not until 5 April 1893 do we find W. S. L. settled aboard *Mercury*.

On 18 December 1895 *Mercury* was ordered home and in his letter of 11 January 1896, W. S. L. sets out her probable itinerary, which his subsequent letters prove to be substantially accurate.

14 September 1891–1 February 1893
Letters from HMS *Royalist*
and HMS *Tamar*

From HMS Royalist[15]

14/9/1891
Between Suau Harbour and Samarai

We send the *Ringdove* down to Cooktown tomorrow morning so I will take the opportunity of sending a letter by her, to wish you many happy returns of the day[16] ... My being in this ship complicates my mail so, as all my letters go to the *Orlando* down South somewhere and then have to be sent on to me up here. I forget how far I had gone in my letter to Mother but fancy I had just got to Cooktown. We had a fairly good time there although not half the place Cairns is. The day after we got there we had a Minstrel party on shore, which was very hot and not up to much. A couple of days afterwards we had a cricket match against the town which we won easily, making 107 to their 24. I was run out after making 2 so my average out here is about 1½ at present. In the evening most of us went to a ball given by the Fire Brigade, where I was taken in hand by two girls called Bauer who gave me dancing lessons which were very successful & I danced nearly everything up to about 2 in the morning.

Out here they have a lot of square dances, all different, called Alberts, Caledonians, Fitzroy quadrilles etc. None of our people had the vaguest idea how to dance these things so directly one of them came along we formed a Naval set with the Captain in charge & danced a dance of our own consisting of a figure or two of the Lancers & quadrilles & waltzing whenever the tune permitted, which was great fun but rather surprised the other people.

We left Cooktown a few days ago & came up to Su-a-u harbour yesterday morning. It is on the SE coast of New Guinea. Yesterday afternoon a shooting party of us landed & trudged about in the bush & among mangrove swamps all the afternoon, returning with about a dozen pigeons & parrots. I was lucky to get a brace of pigeons & a brace of parrots. The pigeons we got are like those big chaps half way up the stairs at Davenport & weighed about 3 lbs. My parrots were lovely birds, one green & red, & the other blue and red. We tried for some time to get some black cockatoos that were flying about but they were very wild & we could only get very long, snap shots through the trees which were unsuccessful. We were trading hard during our stay

17. HMS *Royalist*, cruiser third class, of 1833.

18. HMS *Ringdove*. Redbreast class composite single-screw first-class gunboat, 805 tons. (*Imperial War Museum*)

there, getting paddles, spears, nets etc. from the niggers. We use what is called trade tobacco for these people which costs about ⅓ a pound. I got rather a nice paddle this morning for two sticks of tobacco, value about one penny.

We are now on our way to Samarai to coal & meet the *Ringdove*. We shall, I expect, get in at about 3 o'clock this afternoon, that is, in about an hour's time, I was thinking the other day about writing to Max but he is such an awful way off from here, the letters have to go to England first, I think, & then to the Cape.[17] I enclose a cutting from the *Cairns Post* of the ball that took place while we were there. The naval officers, I may say, were not the 'persons in uniform who jumped the best seats'. Well, I am about run dry, I think, so will stop …

15/5/1892
Union Club, Sydney

I was so sorry not to be able to write last mail but forgot all about it. My promotion [to lieutenant] has at last come through, likewise my orders to return home but the date of my departure is not yet settled. I hope that I will be able to get back before Bob and Maud leave for Honolulu. I was really knocked endways when I was told I was going as I always thought it was too much to expect altogether. My great ambition will also be realised of getting a trip in a big mail steamer. Poor Buckle (Lieutenant) is awfully wild as he has been more than his time out here (3 years) and has been looking forward all along to my taking his place when I was promoted. There is not much going on here. I went yesterday to see the finish of an inter-colonial tennis tournament between N. S. Wales and Victoria. Victoria won to my joy as when these people win anything you can hear of nothing else for weeks. We sail on the 10th for Melbourne & hope to get there in time for a great banquet to be given by Lord Hoptown on the

19. Commander John Casement and officers of HMS *Rapid*, a Heroine class corvette of 1,420 tons.

20. HMS *Mercury*, cruiser. W. S. L. was appointed to her at the China Station as of 17 November 1892. (*Imperial War Museum*)

21. W. S. L., December 1892.

23rd in honour of the Queen's Birthday. The harbour is quite empty now as all the ships have dispersed except the *Boomerang*,[18] *Rapid*[19] & *Dart*. I don't know whether I told you that Ethel Brown was down here. I had her off to tea with one of her friends (I forget her name). They appeared gratified, the friend never having been on board a man-of-war before & Ethel only on the *Rapid* … I hope I shall soon be in the bosom of my family although I cannot expect more than a fortnight's leave.

   Ever your loving son,
   W. S. Lambert

From HMS *Tamar*

8/12/1892
At sea

We are about half way to Malta. We got to Gibraltar about 7.30 a.m. Tuesday, and left at 2.30, fresh in time to see our mail coming from Algeciras to the Post Office, which was annoying. I went on shore for a few hours and got some books, tobacco &c. but there is really no choice of doing anything in Gib. if you don't know any people there … We have been having lovely weather until yesterday evening when it began to rain and has done so ever since, more or less.

   It makes life a perfect blank, as you can't smoke without getting your feet wet. People are beginning to arrange great things for Christmas such as a smoking concert and Athletic Sports – which will occupy four evenings. We are shaking down famously on board and are at last feeling tolerably happy. I had a long yarn with Henderson this morning on watch about old Chili times &c. …

   All our dogs are first rate as they got a good run ashore at Gib. I think I forgot to tell you that we have a very nice chestnut horse going out to Capt. Bourke of the *Victoria*.[20] He is a wonderfully tame old beast and is a great pet with the men who give him pounds of ship biscuits to eat.

   Dec. 9th. Well, I must finish this thing off today as we get into Malta tomorrow morning at daybreak. The rain still continues and is likely to do so – I think it is trying to get up an amateur deluge. We are now off Cape Bon, the northern-most point of Africa, about 190 miles from Malta, and consequently have eased down so as to have daylight to go in with. We stay there until next morning, so I hope I get a good day ashore and go to the Opera in the evening.

   I have just written to Kitty, as I want to find out at Singapore what our programme is when we arrive. There is a rumour of our being hulked in the *Victor Emanuel*[21] for about ten days while the old lot pay off but nothing definite is known – if it is true it would suit me down to the ground, as I would have nothing to do and could see a lot of Kitty …

21/12/1892

We are just getting in to Aden so I will send a few lines to let you know I am all right. We will anchor in about half an hour's time (10.30 a.m.). I sail this evening at six. I shall go ashore for a run but believe there is absolutely nothing to do ashore. I will start writing all round the family when I am settled down in the *Mercury* but will confine myself to these notes to you until then … We have got an anchor lottery up for Aden but, alas, my two minutes are just going to start & we are some way off yet.

   Tomorrow our Christmas Sports start, officers & men. They will last over four evenings but I will write about them from Colombo. Halsey and myself representing the *Mercury* have at last established ourselves as quoit champions on board but I don't know how long we will hold the rank. We have not had it oppressively hot in the Red Sea, just hot enough to wear white clothes comfortably, besides which we have been able to keep our ports open in our cabins the whole time. Well, we are just in, so will stop.

I am,
Your loving son,
W. S. Lambert

29/12/1892

Excuse dirty paper but it is the only piece I can come across at present. We get in to Colombo in about three hours & stay until tomorrow morning. We have had splendid weather until last night since which it has been blowing a bit & we have had to have our scuttles closed. We have been having sports ever since leaving Aden from four to six in the evening & finished last night. They helped to pass away the time but were not very thrilling. We have now started a backgammon tournament in which I have just won my first tie. We are not having very hot weather except at night when it is pretty cosy down below with three in a cabin & the scuttle closed. However, the punkahs are going all night so there is a certain amount of fresh air. I don't suppose we shall get in to Colombo until about six this evening as we had to stop just now for about half an hour as the steam steering gear broke down & we had to repair it. Our Christmas day was a very dreary show & most of us passed it slumbering peacefully all day. I suppose you have got my photo by this time taken in uniform. You can imagine our chuckles when you remarked just before I left that you hoped some day I would stroll into a photographers in uniform & be taken. Well, it is tea time so I will close. I hope you are perfectly fit now.

I am,
Your loving son,
W. S. Lambert

16/1/1893
Singapore Club

We got in here last night at about half past five & most of us have been revelling in the comforts of a shore-going bed. We leave tomorrow morning at six, & in eight days, please the pigs, we shall be quit of *Tamar*. We have had the same beautiful weather since leaving Colombo & have been amusing ourselves by playing cricket, quoits etc. Yesterday the *Mercury* played the *Alacrity*[22] at cricket & beat them. Our parson turns out to be a first-rate cricketer which is just what we want as most of us can't play a bit. The *Mercury* only left here on Tuesday (this is Friday) & so will only get to Hong Kong about two days before we do. It is an awful nuisance as it means that the new crew will have to refit the ship instead of the old crowd whose job it really is. I got rather an engaging elephant at Colombo which I will send to Betsy by Kate if possible. It is too hot to write any more so with love to everybody,

I am,
Your loving son,
W. S. Lambert

18/1/1893
Hong Kong Club

The Lambert luck is still showing up very strong as owing to the want of accommodation

22. A fine model of HMS *Alacrity*, a twin-screw despatch vessel built in 1885. (*Science Museum*)

23. A fine model of HMS *Wivern*, a turret ship of 1863. (*Science Museum*)

on board the *Wivern* where *Mercury*'s are hulked I have to sleep ashore at the Hong Kong Hotel where Bill and Kitty are stopping. They are introducing me to all the people they like which is a grand thing for me, a stranger in a foreign land. We are having phenomenal weather now for this place, frost every night, cold winds all day. Not one's idea of the tropics, is it?

Bill and Kitty leave tomorrow at noon in the *Mirzapoor* & are simply bubbling over with joy at the thoughts of getting home. I wrote a lengthy letter to you at Singapore but with my usual sagacity forgot to post it.

1/2/1893
Hong Kong Club

Many thanks for your letter of the 28th. I am glad you liked the photos. I am sorry I did not write last mail but we are in hopeless confusion now. We are living on board the *Wivern* now until *Mercury* is put to rights which will not be for at least two months. I am rapidly becoming quite a society man as I am slowly but surely becoming acquainted with nearly all Kitty's friends out here who are most kind to me. Later on this afternoon I am going to call on Mrs Fielding Clarke who knew Kitty & has been telling somebody that she wanted to see me ... I went yesterday to the Ladies Recreation Club & played tennis with our parson, Hughes. They have got an awfully nice little place and really good courts ...

19 February–16 March 1893
Letters from HMS *Caroline*

19/2/1893

I am afraid I am awfully bad at writing now but must plead inability to settle down. Here I am in the *Caroline* now eight days out from Hong Kong on our way to Shanghai. In an evil moment one of *Caroline*'s lieutenants went sick so I was hustled off almost at a moment's notice to take his place. Our cruise is as follows:

Shanghai, Port Hamilton, Kobe, Yokohama, Nagasaki & Hong Kong, getting back on the 27th of March. It is an awful nuisance to me as I will be away from the *Mercury* just when my cabin is being done up so that I will have no opportunity of having it fixed as I want it & will have to trust to chance. We have had the most poisonous trip up here, pounding up against a strong NE Monsoon. When we were two days out we had to put in to a place called Owick Bay as we were knocking about fearfully & only going about two knots an hour. We stayed there for about eighteen hours & got our lower yards & topmasts down. The wind and sea have been much better since we left there but for the last two or three days it has been pouring with rain & we poor watchkeepers have been wet through every time we were on deck, through oilskins & everything. Thank goodness it is fine today for the first time this trip. Tomorrow we hope to get in to Shanghai & hope to get a couple of nights rest …

16/3/1893
Nagasaki

I can't remember whether I have written since Shanghai or not so I will imagine I have not. Nearly all our sea work may be described as head winds, rough sea and rain. We went from Shanghai to Port Hamilton south of Korea where we only stayed four hours. Thence to Kobe where we only stayed a day & got a run ashore. From there to Yokohama. Here we had quite a spell of four days which was comforting as it was almost the first chance of a night in since leaving Hong Kong. The day before we left, Maud, Hadley and myself rode out to Kaurakura. It is about 17 miles each way, but with a sagacity beyond our years we managed to lose our way & must have ridden at least fifty miles altogether. However, it was a most successful trip & we enjoyed it thoroughly. The Japanese ponies are something wonderful. Our only difficulty was

24. Officers of HMS *Caroline*.

to prevent their galloping the whole way there & back & they finished up as fresh as when they started. My pony was a confirmed puller, consequently my arms were perfectly dead by the time we finished & I was stiff for days afterwards. We leave here on the 18th for Amoy & then to Hong Kong ...

The *Caroline* is a perfect frost. I must say that I like a ship that goes more than 3 when there is a breeze ahead of her. I am at present on the sick list with a bad foot caused by walking up and down the Peak at Hong Kong, but it is nearly right now.

5 April 1893–7 February 1896
Letters from HMS *Mercury*

5/4/1893

I am glad to say that I have at last returned to my own ship & have turned over to my own cabin from the *Wivern*. Everybody is now busy getting their cabins into order, sticking up pictures etc. I got my box with books, pictures etc. yesterday & my house is beginning to look shipshape. Tell Kitty I have chosen the cabin in the wardroom instead of the big one below as it is much lighter & quite big enough for my wants. It is the middle one on the starboard side just by the end of the table where we had tea. I forget where I wrote from last, Yokohama I think. With our usual luck we got into a gale of wind on leaving & had a most miserable couple of days. We spent a couple of days at Nagasaki & I managed to pick up a couple of very decent netsukes but good ones are very hard to get now. From Nagasaki we went to Foochow & Swatow & thence on here & I joined *Mercury* again … I have been on the sick list since I got back with a foot which is an awful nuisance. This is the second time the same foot has laid me up in the last month. However, a long rest will put it all right. The *Daphne*[23] has just arrived so I am once more united to Watson whom I daresay you remember. He saw the Bobs at Honolulu and Bob lunched in the *Daphne*. No more now,
    I am,
      Your loving son,
        W. S. Lambert

21/4/1893
Hong Kong

Many thanks for your last letter and for the splendid bonus which was a most glorious surprise. I will be able to start perfectly fair now & should be able to make a large profit on my income out here as living is very cheap.

    Things are jogging along very much as usual out here. I am at present suffering severely from golf fever & spend nearly all my days off duty at the golf links at the Happy Valley. I am beginning to get quite good at it. Tomorrow I am lunching with Captain Callaghan & going golfing directly afterwards which is good business as he really is one of the very best. We had the annual mobilisation last week of the *Wivern*, *Tweed*[24] and six torpedo boats which gave us a real hard job of work. I got appointed to the *Wivern*. We went round the other side of Hong Kong & had to try

& hide ourselves in some bay from the torpedo boats. The first day all went well but the second night we were discovered & torpedoed so to all intents & purposes your gallant sailor boy is no more. We had rather a nasty accident during the trip. Leatham, a Lieut. from the flagship, in trying to save a man from getting his foot jammed in pulling up the bulwarks (which are knocked down for firing) had his own little finger taken clean off just above the knuckle. I expect Bill will understand how it was done. He did not mind a bit but everybody else was rather disturbed about it. We are still in the dockyard hands & don't expect to leave here until the beginning of June …

Next week we are giving a dinner to the Shropshire & Hong Kong regiments. We are going to rig up a long table on the poop & dine there as we are rather cramped for space in the wardroom … We are losing our marine officer, Hobbs, in about a week's time as he is invalided home. The marine from the *Caroline*, Daniel, is coming in his place. We are very sorry to lose Hobbs as besides being a particularly nice chap he is a good all-round athlete and sings and plays the banjo very well. However, Daniel is a very good sort indeed but does not shine in sports. Morrisey is going very strong & well & often yarns about the good times he used to have on the river with the Theobalds.

By the way, I was talking to a man in the Shropshire the other day & it eked out that he is a South Welshman & knows Swansea & the Baths very well. His name is Howell …

With love to all hands,
    I am,
        Yr loving son,
            W. S. Lambert

24/5/1893
Hong Kong

Very many thanks for the most welcome help you sent me in my penury. It came just in the nick of time as we are sailing in a week's time for the Pescadores & I would not have even had my month's pay to square up here before leaving. We are going to the Pescadores to put up a monument to the people drowned in the *Bokhara*. I am sending this mail a couple of groups of the officers of this ship which I hope will turn up all right. I am also sending home a little silver sugar basin to Miss Rich. I forgot to send any card or anything with it but I suppose it does not matter much. The day before yesterday we went out for our trial & went about 16 knots. Nearly all of us had guests & we had rather a successful day. My guest was a man called Jordan in the 53rd who was at Burneys with me in '82. Thank goodness we leave for good in a week for Japan eventually where we hope to remain for about a year. The weather here is ghastly, nothing but solid rain for the last five days & very muggy & hot. I have got the Keswick's coming off to tea with me tomorrow. I think they are quite the nicest people I have struck here. I hope next mail to send you yet another photograph (amateur) of myself & Pearson & Halsey with our caddies just outside the golf club. I must stop now as I go on watch in a few minutes …

29/5 … We sail tomorrow at two o'clock so goodbye Hong Kong for about eighteen months. I think the quickest way for you to write in future will be by America after you get this …

28/12/1894
Ketan

Just a few lines to thank you for the Christmas box which I got about two days before, a real good shot on your part. We are now among a lot of islands called the Chosan

Archipelago about a hundred miles south of the Yang-tse & have been here about a week now. We had a very quiet Christmas here, all of us lunching with the Skipper & he & the Warrant Officers dining with us in the evening. The *Mercury* was much admired by the rest of the ships as we were the only one that dressed ship with green stuff over all. At last I believe we are going to leave the Admiral & go down to Hong Kong. The squadron go out for firing on the 2nd then I believe we go south to Hong Kong while the rest go up to Chefoo. It is beginning to get cold & blowy up here now altho' we have had one or two beautiful hot days. Our sportsmen have just returned on board bringing a pheasant & a tiny little hog deer weighing nineteen pounds. There are lots of pheasants here but the cover is so thick that they are very hard to get. Well, I must stop now,

  With best love to the family,
    I am,
      Your loving son,
        W. S. Lambert

1/2/1895
Hong Kong

I am afraid that I have been very bad about writing since I have been here but I seem always to have something on hand, either engagements to keep or some sort of duty to do. I got a letter from you two or three days ago for which many thanks. There seems to be a very fair chance of our getting home before the end of the year as the Captain says that if we go down to Singapore at the end of this month he does not expect us to come North again. We have been quite gay here lately, St George's Ball, a Tarantula dance & a fancy dress ball in the last ten days & the Hong Kong Amateur Dramatic Society have just produced their pantomime. I went to the dress rehearsal a few days ago & thought it first rate, the dancing & singing especially. On the 20th we have the races which last for three days. We hope to remain for them but are not quite sure. I have been chiefly employed on shore in playing golf but am only just getting back to form as I find not playing for a year puts me right back to the beginning again.

  I see a good deal of Laxton nowadays. The poor old chap is awfully cut up at not getting his promotion. It really is hard luck as he has absolutely nothing against him and had a grand certificate as first lieut. of the *Himalaya*.[25] Well, I must knock off now.

  Ever yr loving son,
    W. S. Lambert

25/2/1895
Hong Kong

Very many thanks for your letter & enclosure from Bob received this morning. Be of good cheer, I removed the beard many a long & weary day ago altho' it went to my heart to part with it. We had a short trip last week to Formosa as the Consul at Takau was afraid that the Chinese troops there were going to riot but we discovered that there was no immediate danger & left hurriedly and steamed back here at 16 knots just in time for the last two days of the races. I oddly enough struck a streak of good joss & finished up about $100 to the good. We leave on the 27th for Bangkok & thence go to Singapore so all hands are collecting white clothes etc., as I expect we shall wear nothing else for a long time to come. I hope to send a box of things home by the *Malacca* leaving Singapore on the 22nd of next month but I can't be certain as I find these things never get packed up in time somehow.

I have got a silver mug for C. J. which I am going to send home as I take it he will be in England before me. We have just received a new Sub on board but I have not seen him yet. Well, I must knock off.

Ever yr loving son,
W. S. Lambert

5/3/1895
Singapore

We have left Hong Kong at last & taken on as Senior Officer here. We arrived here yesterday morning & are at present moored alongside a wharf coaling so excuse dirt. We had a first rate passage down, quite calm & going thirteen knots all the way. We stay here until about the 25th & then go up to Bangkok for a fortnight or so. It is quite a pleasant change to get into whites & hot weather again after all the cold & beastliness of the north. We hope now that with any luck we may not go North again but meet our relief here & go straight on home but we have no real news as we don't even know who our relief is. We have been wildly energetic on board since leaving Hong Kong. Morrisey & myself have been going in for a course of boxing singlesticks & Indian clubs every evening & before breakfast & are rapidly becoming young Sandows but are simply covered with bruises from the sticks.

Oh! by the way, if you should be happening along Regent Street way I wish you could tell Wein (!) to send me out a couple of hundred of my cards. He has the plate. Also I should be very glad of the last new *Brassey's Annual*. No more now.

Ever yr loving son,
W. S. Lambert

25/3/1895
Singapore Club

I am afraid I have been very slack about writing since I have been here so here goes before we leave. We are off this afternoon at four for Bangkok & shall be away about a fortnight. The Skipper has got leave to take Mrs Fawkes up in the ship so we shall be a regular family party. Most of us are rather annoyed at having to leave here, just as we are beginning to know people as the only reason Fawkes has for going up to Bangkok is that de Bunsen the chargé d'affaires there has asked him & Mrs P. to stay a few days. The ship, I may say, has to remain outside the bar more than thirty miles off. However, I hope to get a couple of days leave & get a look at the place.

The heat here is appalling and at present I am a dripping mass. One can do nothing until about four & then we play golf or tennis until dark. The Captain has a very nice house here & we have a standing invitation to tennis there whenever we feel inclined. What ghastly cold weather you must have been having at home. I think the North Pole must be drifting towards England or else the Gulf Stream has struck work. Well, I must knock off. Excuse bad writing but I am afraid to touch the paper with my hand or I should leave pools on it.

Ever your loving son,
W. S. Lambert

7/4/1895
At sea

I am just writing a few lines to pass away the time before dressing for breakfast. It is so hot in my cabin after the sun gets up that I generally turn out at about six every morning

& knock around in pyjamas for an hour. We are now on our way back to Singapore where we arrive tomorrow (D.V.) in the early morning. We only stayed for a couple of days as the cholera was supposed to have broken out. In consequence Morrisey, Dalgety & myself were the only Wardroom officers who got up to Bangkok & we had to leave before we saw half there was to be seen. Mr de Bunsen is the Minister there now & was very kind indeed as is his wont. Bangkok is a very interesting old place indeed full of temples simply caked with gold & painted all sorts of colours. The heat there was something awful & the mosquitoes worse, I think, than I have ever seen. We returned to the ship with de Bunsen, Capt. & Mrs Fawkes & went to an island called Koh-si-chang about 5 miles from the bar. The King of Siam has a palace on it & on a small island near it the Commodore of the Siamese Navy (a Dane) has a house & we went there really to call on him. Since that we have been jogging peacefully back to Singapore. I really must try & send a box home when we get back as my cabin is full of things of sorts & they only spoil by being kept in this beastly hot damp atmosphere. I simply daren't look at the Chifu silk that I got for the Black & Levett kids. I expect it is ruined by now. I am going to write to Bob soon & incite him to go home as I expect we will arrive about the beginning of next year if not sooner. This, of course, is only rumour. If you come across Admiral Rice you might ask him if he has heard at the Admiralty anything about who is our relief & when she is likely to occur ...

Ever your loving son,
  W. S. Lambert

16/4/1895
Singapore

Very many thanks for the letter & the ever joyous bonus. I am gradually amassing quite a respectable balance at the bank for use on my return ... We are still here doing nothing much except perspire. We stay here now until May 2nd, the day after Mrs Fawkes leaves for England. We shall then go for a tour to Penang, Batavia, Sarawak etc. I believe we do not go North until about July. We are shortly expecting our new Admiral. I believe he is a very peaceably disposed old gent which will be a relief after our present fussy silly little creature.

On the 18th we are playing the Engineers at cricket. I, for my sins, am in the team, but am not very valuable in that line. We saw the *Gibraltar* on her way home the other day.[26] I saw Stokes who you knew I think in *Wild Swan*.[27] He is a Commander now & seems very pleased with himself. We are looking forward every mail now to see our relief brought forward for commission. She is supposed to be either the *Indefatigable*,[28] *Naiad*[29] or one other 2nd class cruiser & we hope they will come out after the next manoeuvres but *quién sabe*! Well no more now. Give my love to all hands.

Ever your loving son,
  W. S. Lambert

1/5/1895
Singapore

Just a few lines as the mail closes in about half an hour's time & I have a lot of work to do. I have now taken on a new job as Morrisey has gone to hospital with a broken rib & I have to do navigator of the ship while he is away. He left at a rather unfortunate time for me as I find all the last month's work has to be done in a hurry. We have been making great friends with the new regiment here, the 5th. On St George's Day (April 23rd) they had a great time. In the morning at 7 they trooped the colours & had a huge breakfast party to follow, everybody in Singapore being asked. In the evening the

Sergeants gave a ball at the Town Hall which was crowded & a great success. It is the great day in the regiment & the Colonel's daughter told me that usually it is kept up for about a week. All the regiments go about all day with white and red roses in their helmets or caps & all the band instruments are covered in roses.

Yesterday the *Mercury* was 'At Home' to Singapore at the Captain's house which has beautiful grounds. I think it went off very well. We had tennis, croquet, lawn golf & a shooting gallery & gave them lots of tea & drinks & I think they went away gratified. We had the regimental band also which was first rate. I believe we go North in June for the summer cruise but nobody knows.

Ever yrs,
W. S. Lambert

16/5/1895
Penang

We have just arrived here in time to catch the mail so will send a few lines. We have been having a very good time in Singapore but after all it is a change for a few days. We had a great Rugby football match the other day at Singapore, United Services *v.* Singapore in which I played. It was really quite nice & cosy in the scrimmages, the thermometer showing 90° in the shade an hour before we started. I think we must have lost 10 lbs each by the time we finished. We won by 3 goals to nothing. We are now hard at work on every opportunity practising for the Queen's Birthday as we have to land our men & march past before the Governor, fire a *feu-de-joie* etc. with the soldiers. On the evening of the 24th the Governor gives a reception at Government House & to our horror we have been told that we have to go in full dress. Goodness knows the place is hot enough wearing white jackets at night but what it will be with a tight padded full dress coat on I tremble to contemplate. I send you a little group taken of a few of us in our smoking room by one of our Assistant Engineers. Also a small selection of stamps picked up at intervals which some of the kids may have use for … We are staying here for four days & then back to Singapore.

Ever yr loving son,
W. S. Lambert

3/6/1895
Singapore

I don't seem to have written for a good long time but must plead the races, a billiard tournament & various cricket matches etc. We only got back from Penang for the last two days of the races but I managed to get away both days. I had a very successful meeting on the whole finishing up about four hundred dollars to the good which was comforting considering the mild extent of my plunging. I also had the comfort of knowing that I was the only winner in the ship. After the races we spent two days outside running torpedoes & doing our prize firing & have settled down peacefully now in our old billet. I went to the Birthday Ball at Government House & nearly died the death as we had to wear full dress & the heat was terrific. I am in now for a billiard tournament at the club but as we all start level & the other five are the best players in Singapore I fear the worst. However, I have beaten one so will not be utterly disgraced. This day week we go for a short trip to a place called Klang about 250 miles off but will be back in about a week …

Ever your loving son,
W. S. Lambert

25/6/1895
Off Samarang Bank, 25 miles from Labuan, Borneo

How does the above sound as an address? We have just arrived here from Singapore as there is a steamer piled up on the rocks here & we have been sent to try & get her off. It seems rather a big contract as not only is her upper deck under water & her bottom full of holes but we can't get within about a mile and a half of her. She is a big 5000 tons steamer called the *St Pancras* bound from Manila for Singapore & England. We learnt the news directly we arrived at Singapore from Malacca & other ports, having been away for about a fortnight. I had a new experience during the trip as owing to Morrisey's being under arrest for absence without leave I had to do navigator which came off very satisfactorily & the Captain was positively fulsome when I went back to my ordinary watchkeeping. We started our tour by going to Port Dickson which is the port of Serenban, the capital of Sungei Ujong. There as many of us as could went up by train to Serenban & were put up & treated royally by various of the residents there. They had not been visited by a man-of-war for years & the place was quite *en fête*. We got there just in time for the second day of the races which were great fun, the only trouble being that one of the jockeys deliberately pulled his horse in the last race. What I objected to was that I was backing the said horse but no matter as I won $25 on the day. We also had a dance at the Residency & a cricket match (badly beaten) & various tiffin & dinner parties. I did not get to bed before 2.30 a.m. during the four days we stayed.

From Port Dickson we went on to Kuala Klang, the port of Kuala Lumpur, the principal place in Selangor. To get there you have to go up a very narrow strait about fifteen miles long & not very deep. At one place to my surprise & horror the leadsman sung out 'And a half three' or 21 feet. As the ship was drawing 22 ft 3 in it really did seem as if we were getting close to the bottom, but she slithered right through the soft mud & no one knew any better. From Klang a party of us went up to Kuala Lumpur by steamer & train & most of us put up with the Resident. Here again we stayed about four days & had a great time. The Resident gave a dance, we had a rifle match (a tie) & a cricket match (badly beaten) & a football match (just beaten by 2 goals to 1). On the last day of our stay we got up at 5 & went shooting after pig & deer in the jungle. We were out for about six hours & got two deer & a pig. I was unlucky & got no shot at all but our Sub, Youl, got the pig. The deer were got right & left by a man called Scott who has been to every shoot there for three years & these two were the first shots he had fired.

From there we went back to Malacca where we only stopped a couple of hours & then on to Singapore where we anchored just in time to get it up again, go alongside the coal wharf, take in 150 tons of coal & off to this place. In consequence we have not got any mails for over a fortnight, & goodness only knows when we shall, as the steamers between S'pore & Labuan average about three a month & one started just before us. Well, I must knock off for the present & finish when there is an opportunity.

26th. Labuan. We got in here last night & found that a steamer is leaving for Singapore this morning so I must close this at once. We stay here about a couple of days probably after which our movements are shrouded in mystery. I enclose a few stamps.

Ever your loving son,
W. S. Lambert

13/8/1895

Many thanks for your last two letters received at Singapore a few days ago. I don't think I have written since we went to Batavia so will start there. We were there altogether for about a week, most of which I spent in Batavia, some miles by train from where you land.

It is I think one of the quaintest places I have ever struck. The people never dress until after tiffin about 12.30 wandering in to that meal anyhow. The ladies come in dressed in a chemise sort of thing & a sarong which is a sort of calico thing that reaches from the waist down to the ankles. The men generally use a pair of sort of Christy Minstrel pyjama trousers & a white calico tunic. After tiffin everybody goes to bed until about four or five when they dress & go out, the ladies in low evening dresses as a rule. The people of the place were very good to us & we had an excellent time. We played them at cricket with the usual result, making 54 against their 338 but we are getting used to being beaten. On the 2nd we went to a grand ball given in honour of the Queen Regent of Holland's birthday. It was a very swagger affair but the heat was awful especially as we had to go in epaulettes & so forth. We only had a few days at Singapore and came on here & wait for the arrival of old Johore. The latest about him is that we have to hoick him out of his present coffin while he is on board & put him into a Malay coffin. I do trust the old gent has been properly embalmed. Well, no more now. With love to all,

 I am,
  Your loving son,
   W. S. Lambert

3/9/1895
Penang

The mail closes in about an hour so I will just scribble a few lines. We are now waiting for the funeral of the Sultan on the 9th, having brought him down from Penang a few days ago. He came alongside from the mail steamer with a procession of boats with the fort firing minute guns & we hoisted him in & put him into a little house made of white calico on the quarter deck decorated with his crest, a crescent & star, in silver paper.

When we got down to the New Harbour at Singapore we were met by the Governor in his yacht & a lot of steam launches & steamed slowly through in procession, followed by thousands of Malay boats with long white streamers for mourning. We took a lot of Johore officials on board & went on to Johore while they prayed at him. When we got there we put on full dress (temperature about 88° in the shade) & received the Crown Prince on board who went & wept on the coffin & then landed again. We hoisted him out directly afterwards & took him ashore & he was carried up to the Palace preceded by the crown regalia & the band followed by the Crown Prince, all the big bugs of the place & as many of us as could land. After putting him in the room prepared for him all hands prayed & wept over him for about half an hour & then the whole party adjourned to another room & consumed sandwiches & drinks.

By the way, just before leaving Penang I had a few days leave with an old gentleman called Vermont in Province Wellesley & had a great time. He is the proprietor of a sugar estate & has about 13,000 acres under cane. I had a first rate time & found out all about sugar making from beginning to end. We are all sorry to leave Penang just now as the snipe are just coming in & it is the best place in the world for sniping. Latest news says that the *Immortalité*[30] is commissioning in November to relieve us so you may see us home about March. No time for more.

 Ever your loving son,
  W. S. Lambert

11/9/1895
Singapore

I have just missed the last mail but am going to make certain of the next one by writing early. We came back from Johore on Monday the 9th having successfully proclaimed the new Sultan & planted the old chap on the Saturday. I am afraid I don't know much about it as of course I had to stay on board & keep ship & all one could get from the people who went were shouts for long drinks & very forcible remarks about the heat. However, I will get a paper with the account of it all & send that along. The Sultan presented all the officers on board with silk sarongs. I am sending mine home to you by parcels post this mail & also the long promised 40 yards of Chefoo silk for Janet & Nellie. I dug the latter out this morning & found to my surprise that it was not entirely consumed by moths & silver fish, in fact was as good as new. I don't suppose it will be any use when it does arrive but no matter.

We are, I believe, to stay here until the end of the month & then go up to Bangkok for a trip. It is a blessing to get a little peace & quiet for once in a way.

Sept. 15th. I was rather premature in my last remark as the good ship *Mercury* sails for North Borneo, Saigon & Bangkok this afternoon. I, however, do not sail in her as I am at present vegetating in hospital with another go of rheumatism. Personally I am rather glad than otherwise as I hope to come out in ten days or a fortnight & the ship goes away until October 18th so I hope to put in about a fortnight's leave. I have got an invitation to stay at the Barracks with the officers of the 5th & please the pigs will have a first rate time. I suppose all you people are still up in Scotland. You are a-going of it? I am quite resigned to seeing you dashing round Battersea Park on a bicycle when I get back. We are still very cheery up here in the officers' ward altho' the society is a trifle mixed. We have only one lunatic at present & he is quite harmless. However, probably we shall get some DT cases soon as the complaint seems pretty prevalent in these parts. I suppose you have got the Bobs at home now. Tell Maud it was rather low down not letting a fellow know when they were starting. I have not written to Chile for ages as I had not the faintest idea when they were starting so it is her own fault.

… There is no more news about our relief but I think the *Immortalité* yarn was from pretty good authority so about March should be our date of arrival home. It is a beastly time of year to get home but thank goodness it is early enough to prevent our leave being tampered with by those awful manoeuvres. The skipper is trying all he knows to get up to Japan before we go home & we are all with him bar some of the old married men. I should much rather stay here another couple of months if only we could spend them up there quietly by ourselves, as I have purposely avoided getting anything in the silk & china line, thinking we were sure to have at all events a few weeks there in our last year. Well, as you may suppose, there is no particular news obtainable up here so I will shut up. Don't think there is much the matter with me 'cos there ain't.

Ever your loving son,
W. S. Lambert

21/9/1895

Still in hospital but hope to get out in two or three days as I am quite convalescent. I am beginning to get very sick of this show, nothing to do but get up, sleep, read, eat & go to bed again. I have been foiled in my hope of getting some leave by the *Mercury* going away by a telegram from the Admiral telling us to wait here till further orders. It was very lucky for the Skipper that the said telegram arrived as the day before we ought to have started he fell down the Club steps & hurt himself badly. He is up at Government House now till he is better, much to the joy of the people on board. We are living in hopes that our Admiral is sending a ship down to relieve us & let us get up North but so far have heard no news.

Lady Mitchell the Governor's wife came to see me the other day. She is a dear old soul & we are all very fond of her. We know them pretty well as we brought them back from Batavia the other day. There is not much news I am afraid except that a subaltern in the Engineers has eloped to Colombo with the youngest daughter of the Colonel of the regiment. I wish her joy of him as he has not got a cent beyond his pay & has a reputation for getting engaged to girls & then breaking it off. Our only excitement up here is watching the golf between 4 & 6 as one of the holes is just outside. There is a beautiful bunker in the shape of some pailings [?] just about 120 yards from the tee & right under our noses & we often get some excellent sport provided for us. Well, paper & news is finished, so will shut up.

Ever your loving brother,

W. S. Lambert

6/10/1895
At sea

I don't know when I shall have a chance of sending this but it is just as well to make a start. I am perfectly well again & just left hospital in time to go away in the ship. We are now on our way to Bangkok where we expect to stay for a few days & return to Singapore by the 17th. It is a rotten trip as the only reason for it is that the Skipper wants to see Mr de Bunsen & it seems rather quaint to go sixteen hundred odd miles to pay a call. The Skipper himself is on the list now with a smashed up knee, having fallen down the Club steps a couple of weeks ago. People have been inclined to make rude remarks about it but I fancy all was well with him at the time.

Everybody is looking forward now to the races at Singapore which start on the 22nd. We will be just in time for them. I am living in hopes that I shall have as good a meeting as last time when I won $400 but alas, that sort of time doesn't come every day. What times you must be having now with the Bobs at home again. When I get back we will be able to muster the entire clan for the first time for many a long year. We have had no fresh news of our relief so are still praying for February & the *Immortalité*. We are all so utterly sick of this part of the station. We have been down here now for nearly eight months in the sweltering heat & everybody is beginning to go sick with fever, boils & various loathsome skin diseases. We have now about twenty-five on the sick list not counting half a dozen in hospital. However, we hope the Admiral will be down here next month & that he will take us up North with him shortly after.

Oct. 10th. Off Bangkok Bar. The mail goes out today so I will close this up. I am sending a few stamp for the collectors thereof which I think finished all the brands belonging to this part of the world. Most of our people are now up at Bangkok on leave. Our cricket team went up to play this morning. I am staying on board while we are here this time & letting the other watchkeepers go on leave as I had my leave when we were last here. Latest news says that things are not going on well up north over this missionary slaughtering row so we are now living in hopes that we may be called up to China at any moment.

With love to all,

Your loving son,

W. S. Lambert

24/11/1895
Singapore

… I am glad the silk turned up all right. It is a marvel to me as all my clothes have been eaten through by ants, cockroaches, silver fish (a peculiarly offensive sort of moth) long ago. We have been quite busy lately. The Admiral came down a few days ago & on Friday inspected us from 9.30 till about 2. It rained briskly the whole time & everybody was in a fiendish temper so I am afraid the report will not be brilliant but no matter, we will be home in a few months & will be able to hoot at the Admiral. The day after (yesterday) we had our first three courts martial since we commissioned. Morrisey, whom Janet knows, was the first case for absence without leave. He was lucky and got off with the loss of six months seniority. Then came rather a quaint thing as directly his case was over he was called on to try the next one as a member of the court, a sudden elevation from the dock to the bench which I should think was unique. The other two were bluejackets but I had to defend one of them which nearly turned my hair grey. However, I was of no use whatever to him & he got a year's imprisonment & dismissed the Service. We are now looking forward with great anxiety to the arrival of the *Undaunted* who is coming down to relieve us.[31] We expect her in about 3 days time when we will start straight off for Hong Kong which will be a most happy release from this beastly hole ...

Nov. 30th. With my usual sagacity I missed the mail last Wednesday & we are now leaving in half an hour for Hong Kong via Saigon so I will close this. The *Undaunted* came in last night. I expect they will be late but here's all the compliments of the season etc. ...

Ever your loving son,
W. S. Lambert

4/12/1895
Saigon

Here we are at last on our way to Hong Kong. There is a steamer going to Singapore the day after tomorrow which will catch the next P&O so I am going to send this by her. I fancy we shall not get a very good inspection report. It is a great pity as our first lieutenant has spent any amount of time & money in trying to get the ship up to the mark & then it is a great cross to find out that it is no good ... We left Singapore on the 30th & got in here yesterday afternoon after rather a dusting from the NE Monsoon. It is a very quaint place but twenty-four hours of it is quite enough as it is deadly hot & you can talk nothing but French. I have been talking the purest Parisian for the last two days & my hair is turning rapidly grey.

Last night we went to a comic opera *La Fille du Regiment* performed at the Government Theatre here. One or two of the company were pretty good but the rest trash. The music, however, was first rate & we were rather glad we went. I am on duty today so cannot see tonight's show *La Traviata* which seems rather ambitious on the part of the company ...

We leave here tomorrow afternoon & hope to get to Hong Kong about the 9th altho' you never can tell how hard this monsoon is going to blow.

I am,
Ever your loving son,
W. S. Lambert

22/12/1895
Hong Kong

I feel awfully ashamed of myself for not having written before to thank you for your most welcome Christmas box. My only plea is hard work. Owing to various people being sick & in hospital & odd jobs outside the ship we have been reduced to two watchkeepers, day on & day off, & I have also to do the navigator's work so am rather pressed for time, as Morrisey who is invaliding home has left a lot of back work which I have to get up to date if possible before the next man comes. We are peacefully settled down here now until about the 8th of next month when, I hope, we will start for Singapore to meet the *Immortalité*. The Skipper says that he hopes to arrive in Portsmouth about the 15th of February so at last the time seems to be getting pretty short. The *Caroline* came in this morning from the North. It has just been broken gently to them that they are to make a sailing passage home round Cape Horn which will probably take them about three months. We are very quiet here now, an occasional dance or so being the only excitement & those I don't attend. I generally spend my days off in the Happy Valley, maltreating golf balls. I seem to get worse and worse every day. We have just heard of the accident to the Prince of Wales. I hope the poor old chap doesn't lose his eye. Well, no more.

Ever your loving son,
W. S. Lambert

11/1/1896
At sea

Here we are at last on our way to Singapore homeward bound, having been suddenly shunted off from Hong Kong at about two days notice. We had quite an exciting time for the last three days. The *Caroline* went off on the 7th, the *Grafton* on the eighth,[32] and ourselves on the 9th, all ships being well cheered by all men-of-war in the harbour. We are coming down at nearly thirteen knots which is a most useful speed & we hope to pick up the poor little *Caroline* tomorrow or next day. It is rather hard luck on her as they expected a good stiff monsoon, instead of which there has been an almost flat calm for this half of the journey at all events. I don't know whether it is any good sending you our programme as we shall be home very shortly after this letter unless detained at Aden in which case goodness knows what may happen. However, this is the latter part of it according to present arrangements:

	Arrive	*Depart*
Aden	January 30th	January 31st
Suez	February 4th	February 5th
P. Said	" 6th	" 8th
Malta	" 11th	" 13th
Gibraltar	" 17th	" 18th
Plymouth	" 24th	

& then on to Portsmouth.

As we have probably to pay the ship off into the Dockyard Reserve I don't suppose we will get on leave for at least a month as the last ship, the *Leander*,[33] took five weeks paying off. My present idea is to try for a short course of Gunnery & Torpedo after my leave is up, chiefly for the Gunnery as I have never been shipmates with quickfiring guns I shall be awfully out of it if I went to a modern ship next. Tell Bob he need not put off any engagements this time as I will have, I expect, 45 days leave due to me on arrival in England instead of only sixteen as last time. We are now the happy possessors of nine Chow puppies which various people are taking home. They amuse themselves by yelling briskly all day & all night & make the ship like a dog show but I expect they will die off before they reach home as one is in extremis already. I don't know whether I told you that our much loved bear Alphonse died in his keeper's arms on Christmas morning. It cast quite a gloom over the ship & his keeper dissolved into floods of tears. However, Dalgety hopes to get another when we get to Singapore.

25. HMS *Leander*. Twin-screw cruiser, second class, 4,300 tons.

14/1/1896
Singapore

Just received your letter of Dec. 20th for wh. many thanks. Mail is just starting so must close. We sail at 6 a.m. tomorrow.

Ever yr loving son,

W. S. Lambert

18/1/1896
At sea

I won't be able to send this till we get to Port Said or Malta but will make a start anyhow. We left Singapore on the 15th & have been having a lovely trip up to now, a good strong breeze on the quarter & calm sea & have been making good at least 13 knots, since we started. We have got fore & aft sail (our little all) on her & it really is helping her a good deal besides keeping the ship cool. I was unlucky at Singapore as it was my day on when we arrived & I only just got ashore for an hour or so in the forenoon & missed seeing all our old friends there. We just beat the *Caroline* into the harbour having given her 42 hours start & now have about half a day's start of them from Singapore as they had turned over their Chinese servants etc. to the *Narcissus* which arrived the same day.[34] We passed our relief this morning at 3 o'clock so now will take all our Chinamen home to England & pay their passages home to China for them when we pay off. They are full of an holy joy in consequence as none of them have been off the station before & are awfully keen about seeing England.

Jany 23rd. We left Colombo yesterday at noon after a stay of about two days. I got ashore the first day & wandered around aimlessly all day but escaped a very filthy coaling which was a blessing. Here we got rid of of our guest, Lord Shaftesbury, who has been taking passage with us from Hong Kong. He left in the Australian mail to resume his duties as A.D.C. to Lord Brassey in Melbourne. He is about my age & seems a very good chap. He said that the *Sunbeam* had a splendid passage out nearly entirely under sail, at one time averaging 250 miles a day for about a fortnight.[35] We are jogging along very comfortably now at about 12½ to 13 knots, fine weather & calm sea, but hope soon to pick up a good monsoon & get along a little faster. We hope to get to Aden on the 29th when we take in 250 tons of coal & get away next morning. The Skipper has brought our programme down to arriving at Plymouth about the 19th or 20th, but it is all guess work as we never know where we may not be detained or for how long.

Jany 28th. We are still wandering on peacefully & hope to reach Aden tomorrow at daylight, coal, & leave the same afternoon. We have been having such a lot of current the last few days that we have been obliged to ease down to about 10½ knots to wait for daylight … We are getting quite aristocratic on board here as the Skipper tells me that he has asked the Marquis of Ormonde to meet him at Port Said & come home in the ship. You won't know me, I expect, when I have got my society manners on.

We are now reduced to three watchkeepers as Dalgety has gone on the list, which is rather a nuisance but no matter, this day three weeks we ought to be in Plymouth. You must let me know the Wodehouse's address so that I can call there on arrival at Portsmouth. We have missed the last two mails through some mismanagement which is a bore as there is sure to be just the most exciting news then.

Aden. 29th. Arrived this morning & just catch the *Caledonia*.[36] We sail at 5 tonight.

Ever yrs,
W. S. Lambert

2/2/1896

I am going to start a few lines in case we get a chance of sending a mail from Port Said. We got to Aden on the 29th & left the same day after taking in 250 tons of coal. I thought perhaps we should find the *Brisk*[37] there with Capt. Rich but was disappointed as the *Cossack* was the only ship there.[38] We had beautiful weather for the first two days out but since that we have had a nasty head wind & sea & were obliged to ease. This morning, however, it is perfectly fine again & we are bowling along at about 12. We hope to get in to Suez at daylight & start up the Canal as soon as possible afterwards. We shall probably have to wait about a couple of hours as we have to be measured & mustered for Canal Dues & the Paymaster has to land to pay them. We also expect to get a mail there.

By my not getting any letters at Aden I expect you have knocked off writing till I get home which is vexing as I forgot to tell you that we go on getting mails the whole way home. We have all been deeply interested in the Transvaal show & were half expecting to be sent off to Delagoa Bay on arrival at Aden.

We went into blue clothing yesterday which seems rather quaint as we have been in whites with the exception of a week or two at Hong Kong for a year on end. I slept under blankets last night for the first time which seems quaint after what one hears of the Red Sea, but I have always said that it was a fraud. Another poor Chow pup has died the death, leaving five only now & I expect the rest will follow soon now the weather is getting cold.

Febry 7th. Malta. Just arrived here in time to catch the mail. I got both your notes (to Gib. & Malta) on arrival … It is my day on today. I have just sent on shore to find out whether the Sam Baths are here as I can get away tomorrow. We sail, I believe, on Sunday morning early.

Ever yr loving son,
W. S. Lambert

• • •

On his return aboard HMS *Mercury*, W. S. L. was appointed, as of 18 June 1896, to a short course in torpedo and gunnery. This would have been in Portsmouth, where the torpedo school HMS *Vernon* and the gunnery school HMS *Excellent* were situated.

Before his next appointment as lieutenant in command of HMS *Boxer*, a destroyer, came through on 18 August 1896, W. S. L. took part in the first large-scale mobilisation exercise aboard the second-class cruiser HMS *Brilliant*,[39] forming part of the reserve squadron. In his letter of 25 July 1896 from *Brilliant*, W. S. L. refers 'to his new appointment in command of HMS *Boxer*, to serve in the Mediterranean'. *Boxer* was one of the earliest destroyers, being of the 'A' class and launched on 28 November 1894.[40] One's first command is always a milestone in one's career, and despite the 'growls' and grumbles about life in such a vessel, it is clear from W. S. L.'s subsequent letters that this was a most enjoyable part of his career in the Royal Navy, and that he ran a happy and efficient ship. Sadly, we have no surviving letters to record his career after 14 August 1897, when he was still in command of *Boxer*. From the Navy List we know that his next appointment was back on big ships, including HMS *Barfleur*, a battleship launched in 1892, and at, the time of W. S. L.'s appointment, lent from the Mediterranean Station to the China Station.

This further appointment to the China Station played havoc with W. S. L.'s health and in little over a year he returned to take up his appointment, dated 23 February 1899, aboard HMS *Duke of Wellington*, an old first-rater of 1852 now doing duty as a depot ship in Portsmouth. A point of interest, perhaps, is that an oak forest of seventy-six acres was cleared to provide the timber for her construction.

26. Eclipse class protected cruiser, 5,600 tons, on the China Station *c*. 1898.

15 July–10 August 1896
Letters from HMS *Brilliant*

15/7/1896
Reserve Squadron

Here we are rocked on the cradle of the deep with about twenty five other poor misguided ships trying to pretend we are enjoying ourselves. We left Plymouth on Monday afternoon & since then we have been wandering about at the entrance to the Irish Channel in a haphazard sort of fashion as if we had dropped something & were trying to find it. Every now and then we have theories on our destination but they are invariably crushed by our turning round & rambling off in the opposite direction. Yesterday all hands said that Berehaven was a certainty as we had been steering straight for it for some time but last night we turned and are now aiming more or less for Falmouth. Where we shall eventually fetch up goodness only knows. I believe we have to get somewhere by Saturday so as to fill up with coal in readiness for our week's war. We have more or less settled down on board now & my messmates seem to be a very decent lot of chaps. The skipper also is all that can be desired, so far at all events & we get on very nicely together.

... We have two of the *Arethusa*'s[41] on board here, Tillard & Bissett, who are both very cross at being dug out for the manoeuvres directly they arrived from the Mediterranean. Well, there is no more news so I will stop & close this up as in these hard times one never knows when the mail may go.

Ever your loving son,
W. S. Lambert

17/7/1896
At sea

I don't know where we are, where we are going & when we will get there but anyhow I will start away a few lines to post on the next opportunity. We passed through the other fleet just before we got to Falmouth on Wednesday & it was a real fine sight, about fifty or sixty ships of all sizes all of a heap. We got into Falmouth on Wednesday afternoon & picked up our mails but no one landed as it was blowing hard dead off shore & we were miles off. The next morning (yesterday) we sailed again & have quite settled down into the usual routine drills all day of various sorts & one's regular watches. I had a pleasing night quite lately, went to bed after ten, turned out for night

27. HMS *Brilliant*. Twin-screw cruiser, third class, 3,600 tons.

quarters at 10.30, played around with my guns until 11.30 & then went to bed until 11.50 when I got up and kept the middle watch until four. We have only half our fleet together now as the other half with Admiral (E.H.) Seymour have gone off I believe to Milford. We thought we were going there too but now we are somewhere SW of the Scilly's [*sic*] & are steering East & told to rendezvous in case of separation close to Ushant, so it looks as if we were returning to Plymouth or thereabouts. Please forward all documents that don't look like bills. I will conclude when we get there.

19/7. 'There' turns out to be Portland where we arrived yesterday afternoon. We are here now I believe until Tuesday or Wednesday when the war will start. Half our fleet is now at Milford Haven & half at Portland & as far as we can gather the object of the other fleet is to prevent our two halves from effecting a junction … I suppose you noticed that poor old Dan Laxton has got his promotion at last. I am afraid it won't do him much good as he is seventeen and a half years a Lieutenant. I had my first bit of exercise since I left this morning, Jones our navigator & myself taking the dingy & pulling about all the forenoon calling on friends in various ships. My stroke, although scorned on the river, was much admired in a seagoing boat (N.B. this last remark is for the benefit of our young friends at the Barley Mow). Well, it is getting late & I have to start coaling ship at four tomorrow morning so I will conclude. I have just sent in an application for a short course of torpedo.

Ever your loving son,
  W. S. Lambert

21/7/1896

There is nothing to say but it is as well to write when there is an opportunity as one never knows when the next may occur. We are still in Portland & according to the latest rumours, do not sail until Friday when war will start. The war will only last five days & then we live in hopes that there will be nothing more to do except our firing, inspecting & paying off. Our skipper says he hopes to be paid off by the 8th of next month. I hope soon to hear whether I can have my torpedo course or not. If I get it & we pay off on the 8th I ought to get about a month's half-pay as the course does not start till Sept. 7th, which will be good business. We are having lovely weather here. I hope it lasts through the manoeuvres as it makes all the difference between a pig's life & otherwise. I wonder did Bob go to the bicycle show at Queen's? It must have been rather sport.

Your ever loving son,
W. S. Lambert

24/7/1896
Torquay

Just a few lines to say that we expect a war to be declared at any moment. We came on here yesterday as Portland is an enemy's port. This afternoon or tomorrow we expect to try to get thro' the enemy & join the fleet at Milford. We are pale but comparatively calm up to date. The only prayers heard relative to the war are that we may be captured at once & sent back to Chatham as we are all sick & tired of this twaddle. They are giving no leave here I regret to say as I should have liked to have gone over to Dartmouth & seen the *Britannia* once more. They say she has been so wonderfully improved since I was there. I don't suppose I shall get another chance of writing after this but can't say for certain. We may be up in the north of Ireland for all I know. That is what I consider the chief beauty of these manoeuvres. Well, I must knock off. Do not grieve for me if I fall in battle.

I am,
Your loving son,
W. S. Lambert

25/7/1896
Torquay

I suppose that before now that you have seen my appointment to the *Boxer*. It was a most welcome surprise to me as I had given up all hopes of getting one until the end of the year. I see in my appointment that I am appointed (excuse tautology) to the *Endymion*[42] for *Boxer*. The *Endymion* is shortly going to the Mediterranean with a relief crew for the *Hood*[43] so I expect the *Boxer* will be one of the destroyers to go out to Malta. I had rather have stopped at Portsmouth but no matter. We have been told today that after the manoeuvres & target practice we are to assemble at Portland to be inspected & dispersed so I expect we shall be paid off by Augt 9th or 10th, which will be a short spell for me as my appointment is dated the 18th. We are now properly at war & leave here tonight at midnight our ultimate destination being Lough Swilly if the enemy will let us get there. I don't suppose there will be any further chance of writing till I get back to Portland about the 31st.

I am,
Your ever loving son,
W. S. Lambert

31/7/1896

There is a slight chance of our getting and sending mails this afternoon so will scribble a few lines on chance. We are now in the Irish Sea about opposite Dublin, steaming down to Portland with the fleet. The war was a great success as our fleet steamed gaily into Lough Swilly & were not seen by the enemy until they were anchored there. We had personally a most bloodthirsty night on Wednesday. It was a first-rate war night, black & foggy & a steady drizzle. We commenced with a stirring contest with some lights we saw which eventually resolved themselves into an inoffensive sailing ship. Next about 4 a.m. we fought an enemy's cruiser, thereby

28. HMS *Endymion*, an armoured cruiser launched in 1891. Edgar class. W. S. L. was borne on the books of this vessel while serving as commanding officer of HMS *Boxer* at the China Station. (*Imperial War Museum*)

29. HMS *Jaseur*. Torpedo gunboat, alarm class, launched 1892. (*Imperial War Museum*)

30. The Simpson Road Racer, from the firm's 1896 catalogue.

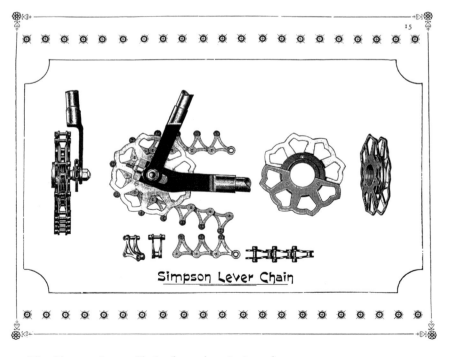

31. The Simpson Lever Chain, from the 1896 catalogue.

bringing up five battleships & two more cruisers so we fled indiscriminately. Next we were discovered & chased by four cruisers who kept us going full speed until the war was up at 8 a.m. Fortunately we had the legs of them & kept outside the mile that they had to get within to capture us. As far as we can gather we were the only ship to meet the enemy at all.

We disperse tomorrow & do our firing & then rejoin the fleet & go on to Portland & then after inspection go on to Chatham & pay off. The latter will not take place until about the 10th, I expect. Well, there is nothing more to say so I will stop! Oh! by the bye we got a piteous signal from the gunboat astern of us, the *Jaseur*[44] asking us if she sent a boat when we stopped for mails, we could let her officers have some food as they had entirely run out, so we have prepared them a case with bread, sardines, pots of soup etc. to keep them going till we reach Portland.

Your loving son,
W. S. Lambert

6/8/1896
Chatham Docyd

We arrived here this morning & are comfortably tied up in the Basin. We do not pay off until the 16th, but I am going to try & get away a few days before if possible. I thought of dropping in at Hayling before joining *Boxer* but it is impossible to make plans before knowing what day I leave. I believe that *Endymion* does not leave until quite the end of the month so I will have a spell at Portsmouth to get my kit together. I propose going to Canterbury today to see the Australians play but don't quite know if the trains suit. Well, there is no news so will stop ...

32. HM training brig *Martin*.

10/8/1896
Chatham

I have just found out that I leave the ship tomorrow morning. My present idea is to go up to town & arrange all my packing & go down to Hayling next day, staying there until the *Boxer* commissions. I have made arrangements with Small to get me some food for tomorrow. If I find however, that there is not much to be done I shall go down tomorrow night. I got a note from Maud yesterday telling me to mention the train I arrive by as they all propose meeting me on their bikes. My bike should arrive today at 33 from Simpson's. I trust my new chain will cause a slight sensation on my arrival.[45] I met Hutchison (late of *Caroline* in Pacific) this morning. He enquired tenderly after you & the girls. He has just been married & is very pleased with himself. I don't think I told you that I dined with Herbert Powley the other day at Portland in the *Martin* brig. Well, there is no news.

    Ever your loving son,
    W. S. Lambert

P.S. The collection of bills at 33 was a best on record nearly a foot high.

21 August 1896–14 August 1897
Letters from HMS *Boxer*

A letter from R. S. (Bob) Lambert, elder brother of W. S. L.:

31/8/1896

I think you would like to hear of my Saturday's trip with Bill on the *Boxer*. I went on Friday evening to Portsmouth and dined with Bill at the Naval Club and after a few games of pool returned to the 'Nut' at about 10.30 p.m. where I slept and Bill passed his first night in his ship. We breakfasted together at the 'Nut' 8 a.m. sharp and walked to the *Boxer* who was next to the *Bruizer*, Halsey's ship.[46] The programme was, originally, adjust compass and have steam trial but alas! we found leaky tubes awaiting us so Bill had to dash off to the C.O.'s to get permission to adjust, at any rate. This he got and out we went with *Bruizer* who was to be swung first and three torpedo boats. To wile [*sic*] away the time we went at full speed to Cowes where the guardship, very impertinently, wanted to know who we were, where from, why &c. I wanted Bill to ask them who gave them leave to stay where they were, but he would not and I did not know how. We then returned and awaited the Staff Commander, who swung us, then after a capital lunch we returned. We were disgusted to hear that Bill will have to sail, probably, this evening, but hope for the best. We got back here in time for tea and Bill stayed the night, going back to ship last night. I do hope the dear old chap will not have to go so soon after all. He was so disappointed about having his visit to you knocked on the head. All the women folk are working like demons to get his curtains &c. done.

 Dear love to all from us,
  Your very loving son,
   Bob

• • •

4/9/1896
Portsmouth

I am afraid that I have been most remiss about writing but the troubles & trials of the last few days seem to have kept me going all day. Today we have been having a Court of Enquiry on our breakdown (the third) but they are still sitting so I do not know the result. I hope they do not blame our engineer as he seems to be such a thoroughly

33. HMS *Boxer*, 'A' class torpedo-boat destroyer, launched on 28 November 1894. 27 knots. W. S. L. was appointed in command as of 18 August 1896. (*Imperial War Museum*)

34. HMS *Bruizer*. She was HMS *Boxer*'s 'chummy ship'. Her wardroom was virtually identical to that of HMS *Boxer*.

good chap all round & is taking these accidents rather to heart. Very many thanks for the tea basket which arrived two days ago. It is really an invaluable thing on one of these ships as tea is the only sort of entertaining that one can go in for as regards one's female friends. I am so sorry I have not been able to get away to see you but I know you understand how impossible it has been. We stay here now probably till Tuesday but there is lots to do & I don't expect to have much spare time except perhaps to run over to Hayling for the night. Well, I must go up to the Rice's for tea now so will stop. They asked me for tennis but as it has been raining solid for the last 24 hours I expect their ground is under water. In case it may interest Bill our breakdown is caused by all the tubes of our foremost boiler leaking.

Ever your loving son,
   W. S. Lambert

14/9/1896
Royal Naval Club, Portsmouth

Many thanks for your letter of yesterday. I am going out tomorrow morning for my trial & then will go on to Plymouth as soon as possible as Admiral Rice wants me to be ready for sea & away to Plymouth as soon as possible …

I had another chance of benefitting my ship's company today, as they were all stone broke & the parent ship (*Endymion*) is now nearly at Malta with all our papers so I had to advance them what they wanted (£46 10s). Fortunately I have a large balance & can let them have it as if they had a poor brute worth nothing but his pay they would have got nothing.

Ever your loving son,
   W. S. Lambert

29/9/1896
Plymouth

Here we are at the first stage of our journey in safety. We left Portsmouth on Saturday & went along pretty comfortably to the Start where we met a snorter & as the ship seemed to prefer being under water to being on top I put back to Dartmouth & tied up to a buoy. The next day was beastly with a falling glass so I remained there quietly & ran round in comparative comfort yesterday morning. They did us real well in the *Britannia* & I went all over the ship & up to the field, kennels &c. which I had not seen since I belonged there. We remain here until Saturday & go out with the *Flora*.[47] Everything is shaking down very nicely on board & I think we are certain to have a good time. It is a great blessing to have had all this bad weather as I think this year's allowance must be nearly expended by now. I have just sent my Sub on four days leave as he lives round this way & it was rather a bother for him to get round from Portsmouth. Well, it is lunch time so I must stop. Excuse any dirt about this note but we are alongside a coaling hulk & have just this minute finished coaling.

With best love to all,
   Yr loving son,
      W. S. Lambert

3/10/1896
Plymouth

I really think we are off at last. We go out to the Sound at noon today & off to Gib with the *Flora* as soon as she has finished her trial. It is a lovely day so I hope all the bad weather is over & that we have a fine passage. We should get to Gib. if all is well by, I should think, Tuesday night, stay a day or two there for coal etc. & then off at once to Malta. I see in the papers that the Turks are guarding the Dardanelles with ten torpedo boats so there is something to go on in the destroying line should the Sultan get restive ...

7/10/1896
Gibraltar

We have arrived here safe at last after many little troubles & trials. We started away with the *Flora* in beautiful weather but next morning it was rather jolty & damp & altogether beastly which lasted two days. I never drank so much seawater in all my life. Hayling bathing wasn't in it. Adding to this the fact that I was deadly seasick, nearly always wet through & sleep in my cabin at sea is practically impossible I must own it was not a cheery time. The morning before last we discovered that our coal would not last so the *Flora* took us in tow with the only result that she parted our only chain cable whereupon we went into Vigo, stayed the night, coaled next morning & got away about 8.30 a.m. yesterday in lovely weather. This morning the captain of the *Flora* thought I had better get in here before dark so I went off from him at six & got in here about 5.30 having averaged 18.9 knots since leaving him. We tried to do it at 21 knots but discovered that if we kept it up we should be left 20 miles outside with no coal which would have been awkward so reduced to 18, finishing up with a grand spurt with yards of flame coming out of the funnels alongside the Rock. I am going to send you a telegram tomorrow morning to let you know I am still in the land of the living.

    Ever yr loving son,
      W. S. Lambert

35. HMS *Flora*. Second-class cruiser of 1893. Astraea class. (*Imperial War Museum*)

13/10/1896
Malta

We arrived yesterday morning after a lovely trip. I haven't written before on account of hard work as since I have been in it has been a long & weary tramp around after Admirals & dockyard officials with intervals of coaling ship, getting the mast down for scraping etc. The Admiral tells me that we are not going to sail for Salonika until the 24th so I hope to get the ship fairly clean by the time we leave. We are all getting on first rate on board & I hope to have a first rate time out here. I have managed to persuade the Admiral here (King) that an escort to Salonika is quite unnecessary & that I am much better by myself so now he has promised to let me go on my own hook. Well, there is really nothing to say so I will finish, especially as it is nearly dark. I am sitting on the upper deck now entirely clothed in white duck & am feeling hot. Think of that, you poor people in England.
　Ever your loving son,
　　W. S. Lambert

23/10/1896

Just a few lines to say that we have got sailing orders for Salonika on Monday 26th when we will at last join our parent. We are in an awful state of dirt & confusion on board & digging out like Trojans but it is impossible to try to get the ship clean until we get the workmen out of her. It is simply deadly hot here as we have had a scirocco blowing for the last few days. We are now fitted up with any quantity of awnings, awning curtains & sidescreens to keep the sun off so I expect we shall be able to keep rationally cool. I shall be awfully pleased to leave this place which I loathe. I have been on shore three times all told & don't think I shall bother it again. Thanks much for the book which I like very much as far as I have got. Thank Bob for the tie clips which just arrived in time to save me from suicide. Well. I have to go & hunt Dockyard Officials which is my regular morning's sport.
　With best love,
　　Your loving son,
　　　W. S. Lambert

Excuse dirt but it can't be helped.

4/11/1896
Malta

There is nothing at all to say but I will scribble a few lines to say I am still alive. We went out yesterday for a trip & fired part of our quarter's allowance which served to waste time & gave us a breath of air. We have had about four days' scirocco lately which leaves everybody a limp rag. It has been deadly hot all day today. 85° in the shade about three this afternoon. It is just cooling down a bit now (sunset) & I am writing this in a deck chair on deck. I haven't been able to go biking yet as I find I have always something to do until about sunset & it is no good going for a tour in the dark. The ship is at last beginning to look white so I hope to have her photo'd shortly as also my gallant crew. The ones taken at Portsmouth were no good at all. If my four worthy sisters will state whether they prefer me with my cap on or off I will send my photos along. I forgot to send them before leaving England. Tell Nellie that I will bring her a goat back with pleasure & that there seems to be a particularly fine crop about now. Thank Maud for letter received today. It may interest her to hear that one of my boilers gave way yesterday (a leaky tube) but all is now well again.

Ever your loving son,
W. S. Lambert

5/12/1696
Malta

Very many thanks for the Xmas box. I at once made arrangements for painting the ship once more. I got a letter from Nellie this morning with anxious enquiries as to the nature of a Maltese bulldog. I regret to say that my first attempt at dog keeping was not a success as the poor little brute came on board very seedy & altho' I sent him on shore a couple of days after he died the death the other day. I have now a five months old puppy who is a perfect treasure but a benighted fool. The brand of dog is or looks like a mixture of bulldog and bull terrier, my pup being a dark brindle. I hope he lives through it as he is a pleasing soul. We have just defected all our boilers so goodness knows how long it will be before we leave Malta, not till February I should think …

16/12/1896
Malta

I am afraid that I have been rather amiss lately in writing but the races have been on which has been interesting me a little too much. We have had two days of them altogether – I regret to say that I have made about £30 out of the too confiding public. Many thanks for the book received the day before yesterday; I read it the same day & liked it very much. There is really no news in this hole so I cannot write a brilliant letter. We are here now till the end of January as all our boilers are being retubed. I dined the other day with the new Commander-in-Chief, Hopkins, seems to be a cheery old bird. His flag lieutenant is Sandman whose father owns the big house at Hayling next to Lennox Lodge. I had a long yarn with him on the subject of Hayling, about the old ferryman & various people about the place. I have sent you along a little pen tray which I expect you will have got by the time this arrives. The puppy continues to flourish & enjoys life thoroughly. The monkey & he are great friends only rather cool at present as the monkey put his hand into the pup's mouth just as he was snapping. I haven't taken him out biking yet as I'm afraid of losing him.

Ever yr loving son,
W. S. Lambert

12/1/1897

Many thanks for the letter & bills, especially the former. I am glad you got the card. It is the only photo of *Boxer* extant at present as I can't get one taken until we are out of dockyard hands because the *Bruizer* being lashed alongside us practically would spoil the picture so the man says. I have had groups taken of officers & men & expect the proofs daily. I think they will be good as the same man made some splendid groups of *Bruizer*'s. I hope they are a success as I want you to have a good picture of the puppy. I have not given him a name yet but he answers to ''Ere' so I think I shall let it go at that. I have not decided yet whether he is only a consummate fool or a fiend incarnate, the latter, I think. His favourite food is boots which he chews & then hides in his kennel.

I am living a very pleasant life at present. I hardly ever land in Valetta but go to the canteen & play bat fives nearly every afternoon from two to five by which time

I am usually tired & go to bed early. I met Carden the other day, he is navigator of the *Theseus*.[48] He enquired after the family in general. Well, it is nearly midnight so I will go to bed.

Ever your loving son,

W. S. Lambert

P.S. In the photo of *Boxer* Copleston & myself are forward on the gun platform. Copleston is dressed in a duffle suit which is a sort of thick fearnought & looks white.

17/1/1897
Malta

I am afraid I have been sadly remiss in writing lately but I hope to be better now the bookwork for the end of the year is nearly over. I have been nearly off my head what with pay, ledgers & all sorts of returns about which I am absolutely ignorant. Well there is nothing doing here much. The *Forte*[49] & *Theseus* left here yesterday for Gibraltar & everyone thinks they are going on to Benin about this massacre which has sent them off in great spirits. I wish they had wanted a destroyer or so.

The proofs of our photos have arrived & I have just ordered about sixty for the whole ship's company. I shall send you half a dozen copies of each which will do for yourself, 4 sisters & Maud but I don't suppose they will be ready for some time. I believe they are going to hurry us off to our parent ships as soon as possible which is a blessing but I don't think we can get away for about a month. I see a good deal of Halsey these days as he is close alongside. We play fives nearly every afternoon & exchange meals a good deal. He improves wonderfully on acquaintance & has an aggressive way of being in rude health & spirits on all occasions. Bed time has arrived so I will knock off.

Ever your loving son,

W. S. Lambert

15/2/1897
Khania Bay, Crete

I am afraid I have not written for some time but what with sea trips & preparations for war I have not had much chance lately & the mails here are very uncertain. I am sending them by a French cruiser to Smyrna tomorrow morning. I left Malta last Thursday & got up here next day. The Rear Admiral got very angry with me as I had very little coal left but all is well now as I told him that I had been begging the authorities at Malta to dock me for more than six weeks in vain & my bottom is filthy & our coal consumption is twice what it ought to be. We have been in here ever since watching the Christians & Turks firing at one another, being ourselves, to say the least of it, bored. I was inspected this morning by Captain Prothero, the Flag Captain of the *Revenge*[50] to see if I was ready for action & he harangued me at great length about the necessity for my being ready for war at five minutes' notice but I think there is not the remotest chance of anything happening. I regret to state that while the *Revenge*'s are bristling with warfare, the *Boxer*'s remain quite calm, the only thing bothering us being the difficulty in getting food, chiefly bread. I don't think the Greeks can be such fools as to run up against Turkey, Russia, Austria & Italy all at once. The combined fleet landed about 500 men this afternoon to protect Khania, poor brutes, as they will have a pig's life on shore & no kudos. We have a great fleet here now, about 20 battleships & a lot of cruisers & small fry. It looks just like a Spithead Review, salutes

36. HMS *Bruizer*, sister ship to HMS *Boxer*. Commanded by Lt Halsey, a friend of W. S. L.'s from his *Britannia* days. He became an admiral. (*Imperial War Museum*)

37. Officers of HMS *Bruizer*.

38. W. S. L. takes HMS *Boxer*, white-liveried, out of Malta for Greece, 7 February 1897.

etc. going on all day. I wish there was a chance of our going out after the Greek torpedo boats but I am afraid it is no go. Prince George of Greece is in a yacht in charge of 4 torpedo boats round the coast & it would be very soothing to catch him & bring him back in triumph. However, it is no good hoping as I am certain myself that it will all end in smoke. It is such a blessing to get away from Malta & to sea after all this time as here one feels wonderfully fit, having a cold crisp breeze off the snow blowing on you instead of the damp clammy atmosphere of Malta. Well, it is half past eleven now so I will to bed. I sent you & Jannie some oranges before I left which I hope have turned up all right.

    With love to all,
      Ever your loving son,
        W. S. Lambert

25/2/1897
Canea

I am starting a letter now because one never knows when mails are going for England until about half an hour before they start & even then we are pretty busy nowadays and cannot take advantage of our chances. I got a letter from Maud yesterday which I answered in time for a mail. I don't know whether it will be legible as we were rolling hideously and even now we are keeping up about fifteen degrees each way which keeps my chair sailing cheerily about my cabin. What irritates me about lying here is that the battleships remain at anchor and do not ever go out & the wind & swell do not affect them at all. Yesterday morning we came in after patrolling all night with a fresh breeze & lumpy sea which kept us knocking about very wet. We got in about 7.30 in the morning & anchored & the flagship told us to send a boat. I did so – consequence I got called names because my boat & its crew were dirty as they had every right to be, poor brutes. Luckily I was not sent for as I was the pick of the basket, not having had my clothes off since the night before. I am sorry I have been bothering you with these growls but put them down to the idiotic way this show has been carried out all through. We might have wiped these Greeks (or the Turks – I don't care which but the Greeks for preference) off the face of the globe a fortnight ago but the Powers go on shilly-shallying, so much that we don't get any forrader at all; in the meantime we destroyers are doing all the work, living a perfect pig's life & getting all the abuse. However, we have at last got to our parent ship & I am getting a lot of things done that I could not manage at Malta.

... Well, I must go to bed as it is 11 o'clock & I could not sleep last night for knocking about & had no chance of going to bed the night before. I will close this when I hear of a mail.

28/2/1897
Suda Bay

We came round here the day before yesterday & find the peace & quiet very soothing. I dined on board the *Dryad*[51] the night we got in, chiefly owing, I think, to a piteous appeal to her, on arrival, to lend us some fresh meat as my puppy on the way round had consumed all we had (about 5 lbs). We have had quite an amusing time today as the Turks have been burning all the Greek villages round the bay today & there has been a continuous fusillade going on since dawn between the insurgents in the hills & the Turks down by the water. About eleven a Turkish ironclad opened fire with her heavy guns on the insurgents but her shooting was infamous & the insurgents apparently did not mind in the least. I got my instructions as issued to all commanding officers today which say that I am to oppose, by force if necessary, all hostile acts on the part of the Greeks, such as bombardment of towns, landing troops or stores, advancement of troops, attacks on Turkish ships etc. Well, I must knock off now as it is just dinner time & the mail closes at 8.30 tonight. It goes by Smyrna so goodness knows when you will get this.

Ever your loving son,
  W. S. Lambert

4/3/1897
Suda Bay

Just a scrawl as we sail in half an hour for Canea. We are doing postman's duty between Suda & Khania (excuse the rather involved spelling of the place) & have been kept on the run for the last three days. We got nine days mails today per *Scylla* with letters from you, Kate, Nellie & Maggie, for all of which much thanks. We had rather larks last night. We got into Khania about 7.30 with letters for *Barfleur*[52] & were promptly sent after a Turkish transport that had sailed about an hour before. We caught her up about 10 & I made her stop. 'You have to go back to Khania,' says I. 'My Turkish Commodore has ordered me to Suda Bay,' says he. 'My English Captain says you have got to go back to Khania,' says I. He scratched his head for a moment & then said, 'Oh yes. I will return,' so I brought him back in triumph.

A Russian lieutenant has just arrived for passage to Khania so I must stop & see to him.

Ever your loving son,
  W. S. Lambert

• • •

From a contemporary press account:

> … It has been noticed that none of the foreigners have such good or large boom boats as our battleships carry. The picket boats are an easy first among the steamboats. The French steamboats have all the appearance of large tubs, iron plates rivetted together, and everything in the boat open and unprotected from the heavy seas that in our boats would sweep over and do no harm. Some of the other steamboats remind one of our own steam pinnaces of ten years ago.
>
> On Sunday afternoon preparations were made by the fleet anchored in Suda Bay to resist torpedo attack. There is no knowing what devilry the Greeks may be up to. The *Revenge*, the *Camperdown*[53] and the *Scylla*[54] moved over to the side of the harbour, making, with the Italians, a long line of ships close in to the shore, and leaving the middle of the harbour clear. Starboard boom net defence was then got out by both battleships, and all scuttles screwed up with deadlights and searchlights got ready. The watertight doors were all closed, and the men, having manned and armed ship, slept at their guns …

• • •

9/3/1897
Suda Bay

Many thanks for your letter received yesterday per *Tyne*.[55] They have just made a signal that mails for England close in half an hour's time which is about the average notice the flagship allows us for writing our letters. We had a job of work the night before last, as the *Ardent*[56] & ourselves had to watch the entrance of the bay & sink any torpedo boats (Greek) which might come in during the night as the Admiral told us that, as time was up for the ultimatum, they might attempt what he described as 'an act of theatrical folly' by running in & destroying one or more of our ironclads. However, Prince George (cowardly brute) never turned up & we had no fun except staying up all night. It was interesting, however, to watch the insurgents & Turks potting one another when daylight came on as we were close inshore & could see them plainly, dodging about the rocks firing. I was woke [*sic*] up at 3.30 this morning as a most animated contest was going on right alongside us, the Greeks shouting & yelling like anything & a Turkish ship firing shells right over the poor *Boxer* at them. I watched them for some time when a ricochet bullet sailed gaily past the ship about 20 yards off us so I retreated in good order to my bunk & resumed my slumbers. We start running despatches between here & Canea this afternoon for four days. Well, no more.

Ever your loving son,
　W. S. Lambert

14/3/1897
Suda Bay

Many thanks for your letter received yesterday & for the ever welcome news of the bonus. I am glad you got the oranges all right. There is no news to tell you of any sort. We coaled yesterday but were shoved off when we had only got half what we wanted to let another ship come alongside the collier, so we have to start again tomorrow morning & start post work at four in the afternoon between here & Carnea. The war

39. HMS *Ardent*, a torpedo-boat destroyer and sister ship to *Boxer* and *Bruizer*. Completed in 1894. (*Imperial War Museum*)

is practically over now but the King of Greece will not withdraw his troops so we have to blockade the island & starve them out.

• • •

A naval officer with the British fleet in Suda Bay, writing on 8 March, said:

> The great value of the torpedo-boat destroyers has been exemplified in these Cretan waters; they have done excellent service in preventing Greek ships from landing stores and ammunition, and also in keeping up communication between the Naval forces along the coast. The destroyer *Boxer*, which acts as tender to the flagship *Revenge*, was sent out from Canea to find a Turkish steamer. The direction of the steamer was not known, but by fast steaming the *Boxer* sighted her in a very short time, and brought her back to Canea. No other nation has such excellent torpedo-boat destroyers in these waters.
>
> Two torpedo destroyers, the *Boxer* and the *Ardent*, with orders not to hesitate to shoot, went outside the harbour and patrolled up and down. Inside these again were three torpedo boats doing the same duty, whilst in order to prevent a torpedo-boat getting in between the ships and the shore the two picket boats of the *Revenge* watched between the *Scylla* – the outer ship – and the shore. The *Scylla* also kept her searchlight going all night across the harbour. No attack was made by the Greek torpedo-boats; but all the same these preparations will continue until a firmer state of peace is established.

• • •

The story of our picture in *Graphic* & *D. Graphic* is this. The Sub-Lieutenant in the *Revenge* who made the sketch knew full well that the *Bruizer* had made the capture but said that as the *Boxer* was the *Revenge*'s tender it was only playing the game to say it was us. Well I have no more to say. Thank Betsy for her letter & the picture of herself & Jackson. My puppy has consumed 4 lbs of pork since last I wrote. Tell Betsy that the enclosed stamps are all I have at present & Stamps here is off as you will discover when you have to pay for this.

Ever your loving son,

W. S. Lambert

25/3/1897
Canea Bay

I don't know when we shall have an opportunity of sending letters but will try & make a start. We are now in the full swing of blockade & my particular job is to patrol Canea Bay. However, the Captain of the *Anson*[57] who is my boss does not mind our anchoring for a bit so I am now spending a few hours at anchor off Gonia for lunch etc. We had a great find this morning as we sighted an English steamer rounding the point & promptly dashed after her. She signalled, 'Have mails for the fleet,' so I told her to go to Canea. However, it transpired that she did not know where Canea was so I sent the Sub on board to put her right. She turned out to be a small steamer from Malta which had started on spec with mails & full up with sundry articles of food to sell to the fleet, so we replenished our food supply & sent her on. The Captain of the *Anson* is a good old sort (Mann by name). I interviewed him last night & when I had finished I said that I had to get some bread and gear from the wardroom steward. 'That's all right,' says he, 'I've got lots,' & sent four loaves of bread & a leg of mutton as a cumshaw down into my boat. Good of him, wasn't it? The popular impression here seems to be that our destroyers have done practically all the work since the show started & Capt. Mann says that all the foreigners regard us with much envy & jealousy. This is rather gratifying altho' of course it increases one's work a good deal. I had a great sell yesterday when I was out patrolling as I sighted a steamer towing a schooner & on coming up to her found that she was flying Greek colours. 'At last,' I thought, 'I had a prize' … when the brute hoisted the Austrian ensign at the fore & her captor, an Austrian torpedo boat, came round the corner. All our soldiers, the Seaforth Highlanders, came up in the *Clyde* P&O from Malta. Two hundred landed at Canea & the remaining 400 have gone on to Candia (also called Megalo Kastron & Heraclion). One gets a trifle confused round here as all the towns have about three names which are used indiscriminately. Well, I will finish this up some time when tidings of a mail come along …

27/3/1897. Canea. Rejoice with me for I have been on shore this afternoon for the first time for 45 days. Williams & the puppy & myself went for a long walk round Canea & about half way to Suda are feeling twice the men we were before. There is nothing much to see except soldiers of every conceivable nationality & uniform imaginable & the ruins of the Christian quarter which was burnt down by the Turks. There was a great fight the day before yesterday, the Greeks & Cretans under Vassos shelling & capturing a blockhouse on a hill behind the town. Out of 64 Turks, 17 were killed, 43 taken prisoner & 4 escaped to Canea. The insurgents however, were promptly shelled out of it by the ships in Suda & the blockhouse burnout but whether the Greeks or by the shells is unknown. I had a little show of my own yesterday as when I was patrolling off Gonia at the other end of the bay some insurgents began cheerily firing rifles at me at about eight or nine hundred yards range so when a bullet came plank against my side I thought it was about time to move off as I couldn't retaliate & the sport seemed a trifle one-sided.

I am sending along some postcards, stamps &c. for Mrs Tillotson as Betsy said she wanted some modern Mediterranean stamps. They are all I could get ashore. They don't work for us as our mails go to Malta & there are no Maltese or English stamps to be got, so I am afraid you will have to pay for this burst of eloquence. We are all getting very sick of this show as there seems to be no prospect of anything happening or of any decision being come to. The insurgent leaders say that autonomy is absolutely impracticable as the inhabitants are utterly out of their control & it is quite impossible for them to keep order in the island without the help of some European power (Greece preferred).

Our pets are going very strong & well on board altho' my pup has rather a bad fit this afternoon from running about in a hot sun after six weeks cooped up on board. The monkey & I are the best of friends now. He got a severe shock yesterday, however. He began fishing about in my pockets to see what he could find & discovered my matches (wax). He hauled one out of the box & of course chewed the business end which went off with a loud report in his mouth. He was, I think, the most surprised person I have ever seen altho' it did not appear to hurt him in the least. I am now wearing my last clean shirt & know not what the future may bring forth. All my washing is ashore here but it was landed by the *Ardent* & she has not been round here since & we don't know where it is. My servant fixes up my collars by using rice water instead of starch which is just enough to prevent them from lying flat down but is better than nothing. I hope a mail goes tomorrow so will conclude as we leave at 6.30 a.m. patrolling.

   I am,
     Yr loving son,
       W. S. Lambert

10/4/1897
Suda Bay

There is a chance for letters at 8 tomorrow morning so I will send a line along. We are tied up in here now for a rest after about a fortnight's patrolling in Canea Bay which is a relief. My experience of the merry Christian in Crete is that he has fired briskly at me whenever I have been in range of him. My own private opinion is that the best thing for Crete is to pull the plug out and let her sink for a couple of days & then start colonizing. There have been various little bombardments going on lately round about here but with my usual luck I have kept out of them all. They talk now of most of the ships leaving Crete & blockading Greece which I take it will be just about twice as bad as this as now at all events we can get ashore & have fresh grub every day which would be impracticable off the coast of Greece.

   Well, there is really no news & I am deadly tired as we have been working pretty hard all day, so with best love,

   I am,
     Your loving son,
       W. S. Lambert

16/4/1897
Suda Bay

Only a few lines as I am half asleep & want to get to bed. We are still here waiting for something to happen. I had rather a cheery night last night. I dined on board the

Rodney[58] in the evening & in the ensuing whist we heard a lot of firing at the entrance of the harbour. I remarked, 'I'll bet the *Boxer* will go on tour tonight,' whereat my host scoffed. At the end of the rubber I went on board the *Revenge* to pick up my engineer & was greeted by the flag lieutenant who told me he was just making a signal to *Boxer* to raise steam & go to the scene of action, so off I went, cruised round all night aimlessly & returned this morning about ten having my mess dress except a monkey jacket still on & not having had a wink all night. Really my luck is the worst on record. The *Boxer* has done as much work as all the rest of the destroyers put together & we are the only one who has found no prizes & had no firing to do. *N'importe*, there may be a good time coming. They had a great review of the international forces at Canea yesterday but I could not get away. However, I believe the Seaforth Highlanders were way up on top. Well, I must to bed. With best love,

Ever your loving son,

    W. S. Lambert

25/4/1897
Canea

There is a mail going on the 27th so I will get a letter written in time. We came back here yesterday morning after a peaceful fortnight at Suda & are now doing turns with *Dragon* night patrolling.[59] We were out last night & came in at 7 this morning. We are now very comfortably moored right inside the breakwater of the little harbour here with the stern tied up to the beach. I hope we don't drag as we are only about 10 ft off the rocks. I enclose the programme of the sing-song held in *Revenge* which was a great success except for the incessant chatter of the audience. This was not to be wondered at, tho', as all the foreign officers were asked and, as an Italian told me, it was no good his listening as the talking was much too quick for him to understand. We were specially detained for this sing-song as Williams, my engineer, was performing & also stage managing. We started white trousers this morning, which is a blessing as it is getting awful hot already. The Greeks I am pleased to see are getting a good hammering which gives one hopes that we may see the end of this soon. Well, there is no news,

Ever your loving son,

    W. S. Lambert

2/5/1897
Canea Bay
9 p.m.

To commence with I will apologise for dirt & bad writing as we are waggling badly & I have been on deck for some time (accounting for the dirt). We are back in this bay now again on the patrol but have had a change tonight taking mails round to Kisamo to the *Harrier*.[60] Last night I had my first meal on shore since Feb. 10th, as I dined at a new cafe in Canea which some enterprising Frenchman has started lately. His cooking is pretty bad but a treat compared with ours. We had a beastly time a few days ago with a strong Nly gale which blows right into the bay, so we had to do without sleep for a couple of days. However, I hope at last the gales are over. The Cretans say that they expect this gale every year as it means that the fish have arrived & that afterwards there will be lots of fish & no wind. I bought yesterday in Canea a most beautiful pair of pistols which were put into the market by a woman whose husband had been killed while fighting the merry insurgent. I shall send them home when we get to Malta (Ah! when). I have been told that I have a first rate bargain

40. HMS *Dragon*, 'A' class destroyer. 27 knots. (*Imperial War Museum*)

& the Turk, or rather Anglo-Turk, Major Churchill, who took me to the shop was rather annoyed when I bought them as he said he had been trying to get the best of everything for the last three months & had never come across these which were better than anything he had …

3/5. … There is a mail going tonight so I will conclude. We are back again in the harbour until tomorrow night & I am trying to get some of the dirt off the ship. There seems to be no news at all about Greece or Crete.

Ever your loving son,
W. S. Lambert

7/5/1897
Canea Harbour

I have been rather adrift in my letters lately but I find most of my spare time on my days off is spent in making up for lost sleep. We are doing two days on & two days off with the *Dragon* now which is much better than having alternate days as it gives you a chance of cleaning up a little on the days off. I am by degrees putting some paint on the ship's side now & the port side is at present most brilliant with red lead. There is no news about the trouble out here except that they seem to think at Canea that Vassos has left his original camp in Platoni Valley & is moving on towards Candea but it is all surmise. We are now getting various telegrams about the war but they all contradict one another so it is hard to say what is really going on. I have just come back from lunch at the French restaurant. It is not a very wonderful place but anything for a change. The spelling there is rather quaint however. Herrings were put down as 'Harengs' but the triumph was the Irish Stew spelt 'Harichtout' which I think ingenious. It is getting quite nice & cosy now. I am writing now in a singlet & pair of pants & am damp to say the least of it. Excuse the dirt but my stylo has taken to leaking.

    Ever your loving son,
      W. S. Lambert

22/5/1897
Candia

Mails have been rather off lately as we have been here for the last few days & there is no regular mail service. We had two rather amusing trips yesterday to a place called Rogia with an interpreter to deliver letters to the insurgent chiefs. I landed with him on each occasion & had a long yarn with the boss chief. His chief wish is for the Turks to be chucked out so that he can get back with his people to farm their land quietly as the crops are just coming on. The poor brutes do nothing but clamour for flour as they have had nothing in the way of bread for months past.

    I am going on board the *Firle* directly to try my new gun on clay pigeons & hope to find it a success. It is a facsimile of the one Betsy gave me & which I lost in Corea. Many thanks for your letter & the little animatograph which is most ingenious. We got our mail at 2.30 a.m. which is a cheery sort of time for reading & answering letters ...

6/6/1897
Candia

I have been sold in the mail leaving so often lately that I must start away in time altho' there is really nothing to say. We are carrying out the same old routine visiting the insurgents about twice or three times a week & calling on the soldiers in between whiles. It is very much better than Canea but deathly slow withal. I have been on board for the last few days as I inadvertently placed my cheek against a red hot lamp top which took all the skin off. It is practically well now but it is a poor game & will not be repeated. The *Tyne* arrived this morning with mails & leaves tonight so I must close this ... We called on the insurgents at Khersonisos yesterday but nothing of note occurred. There seems no prospect of our leaving Crete as *Bruizer* has just been sent to Malta broken down & they say that *Dragon* has broken down on her way up here. What a thing it is to be thoroughly efficient.

    Ever your loving son,
      W. S. Lambert

4/7/1897
Malta

Here we are once more in civilization & heat. It is really a treat to get respectable food once more & also to have plain clothes on again after 20 weeks without them. I am turning over to the *Hibernia*[61] tomorrow with the ship's company as it is much too hot to remain up Dockyard Creek in this weather, besides which I am going to paint the ship inside & out. I expect to remain here for at least two months so tomorrow I propose applying for a month's leave & looking you up. I don't suppose for a second that I shall get in but they can only say no. It is simply appallingly hot here now. It is really all one has to think about. I had to leave abruptly just now as I was bitten by mosquitoes about four times in about two minutes including two on the snout & had to go on deck to get cool & make a few remarks on the subject. Very many thanks

41. Officers of HMS *Boxer*. W. S. L., lieutenant in command, stands on the left.

for the books of Nelson which I liked much & find very popular in the fleet. Well, no more now as I have a lot of Service writing to do.

Ever your loving son,
  W. S. Lambert

I will wire if I get my leave.

2/8/1897
Malta

I have been shocking bad about writing I am afraid but I have been rather seedy with earache for the last couple of weeks which rather puts one off. However, all is well now, thank goodness.

Things are very quiet just now & will be worse as the fleet left for the cruise this morning. I hope to leave here & join them about the beginning of September as I want badly not to miss Venice & Trieste. I sent you a picture of *Boxer* the other day, I wonder whether it has turned up. It is not much good but all Malta can supply. We went into dock this forenoon, the first time since Augt 17th. Many thanks for various books received. I must stop now as it is near pitch dark.

Ever yr loving son,
  W. S. Lambert

P.S. My leave, I grieve to say, is quite impossible as I sent the Sub & he won't be back in time.

14/8/1897
Malta (in Hibernia)

I must start away a note while I think of it & try to keep my mail more regularly. I got a letter from Maud yesterday who seems to be getting along pretty cheerily ... There

42. HMS *Boxer*. The ship's company. W. S. L., lieutenant in command, with the dog 'Ere on his knee, is seated third from the left, second row.

43. HMS *Barfleur*, battleship, 10,500 tons. W. S. L. was appointed to her as of 20 January 1898. Unfortunately, no letters from his time aboard survive. This period was his last on the China Station and resulted in a breakdown in his health. (*Imperial War Museum*)

44. HMS *Duke of Wellington* and *Marlborough*. W. S. L. was appointed to the former as of 23 February 1899 on his return from the China Station. It was to be his last appointment.

is nothing going on here of interest except an occasional small regatta. I don't know whether I told you that I capsized with great éclat outside the harbour the other day. I & my pal were picked up by a passing steam boat who towed the remains back & I discovered to my horror that I had lost my ring. However, next morning the owner of the boat came along & said he had found it in the boat when righting her. Lately I have been playing golf every afternoon. I had a most exciting match with an old Colonel & by a superhuman effort at the last hole finished up all even. This afternoon I am going round with the Captain of Marines here. Well, no more now as I must shave & change.

Ever your loving son,

W. S. Lambert

Family Photographs

Above left: 45. W. S. L. in mufti.

Above right: 46. 'Cousin Winnie'. W. S. L.'s wife Winnifred, née Hardy, *c.* 1902. From a photograph in the album of Rear-Admiral William Penrose Mark-Wardlaw, RN.

47. W. S. L. with his father-in-law, Mr Hardy.

48. W. S. L. in Scotland.

49. Mrs Winnifred Lambert on holiday in Scotland.

50. W. S. L. with his sister-in-law Chris Hardy on the Thames near Abingdon.

Endnotes

1. HMS *Britannia*: At the time W. S. L. was a cadet, HMS *Britannia* was an old man-of-war training ship. In 1859 she was at Portsmouth, then Portland, and from 1864 Dartmouth. Early in the twentieth century the present Britannia Royal Naval College was built ashore at Dartmouth.
2. *Wanderer RYS*: Auxiliary steam yacht launched in 1878 and commissioned by W. S. L.'s father, Charles Joseph Lambert. W. S. L. sailed around the world in her in 1880–82. When she passed out of the Lambert family ownership she became *Vagus* (1889-1902), then *Consuelo* (1902/03). She was sold into Admiralty ownership as HMS *Sealark* (formerly, for a short time, HMS *Investigator*). She was sold out of Admiralty service in 1919 in Melbourne. Later, she was renamed *Sea Lark III*, then taken out of service as *Norwest*.
3. *Britannia*: Journal of HMS *Britannia* and later of the RNC, Dartmouth. W. S. L. refers to the pioneer issue in his letters.
4. HMS *Vernon*: RN torpedo school and training establishment, Portsmouth.
5. *Wave/Dapper*: Tenders for instruction of RN cadets attached to HMS *Britannia*. *Dapper* was formerly a 300-ton gunboat dating from the time of the Crimean War.
6. HMS *Cockatrice*: Sloop.
7. HMS *Iron Duke*: Central battery ship launched in 1870. 6,010 tons.
8. *Saucy*: A small sailing vessel owned by the Lambert family.
9. HMS *Triumph*: Central battery ship launched in 1870. 6,640 tons.
10. HMS *Orlando*: Armoured cruiser, launched in 1886. 5,600 tons, 18.1 knots.
11. HMS *Tamar*: Troopship, 1863. Depot ship at Hong Kong. Sunk 1941.
12. HMS *Mercury*: Cruiser, 1878. Renamed *Columbine* in 1914.
13. HMS *Wivern*: Rigged turret ironclad, launched in 1863. 2,750 tons, 10 knots, armament 9" M/L.
14. HMS *Caroline*: Corvette, 1882. Renamed *Ganges*, c. 1908.
15. HMS *Royalist*: Heroine class composite single-screw corvette. Launched 7 March 1883. 1,420 tons, 13 knots, armament 2×6", 10×5". To Australia for eleven years from 1888. Broken up in 1950.
16. HMS *Ringdove*. Redbreast class composite single-screw first-class gunboat, 805 tons.
17. Max: Unknown to W. S. L. at the time, George Maximiano Lambert had died of fever on 31 July of that year. He had been in South Africa since November 1890, gold prospecting.

18. HMS *Boomerang*: Torpedo gunboat of 1892 (Royal Australian Navy).
19. HMS *Rapid*: Heroine class composite single-screw corvette, 1,420 tons. Renamed *Hart*, 1916. Sold for breaking up, 1948.
20. HMS *Victoria*: Turret battleship, 10,470 tons. 17.5 knots, armament 2×16.25", 1×10", 12×6". Launched in 1887. Sunk in collision with HMS *Camperdown* on 22 June 1893 off Tripoli with heavy loss of life.
21. *Victor Emanuel*: Screw ship launched in 1855 as *Repulse*. Renamed. Sold in 1898.
22. HMS *Alacrity*: Despatch vessel, 1885/86.
23. HMS *Daphne*: Sloop, 1889.
24. HMS *Tweed*: Miscellaneous. Launched in 1877.
25. HMS *Himalaya*: Iron, ship-rigged, built in 1853. Purchased as troopship in 1854. 4,690 tons. Hulked in 1896.
26. HMS *Gibraltar*: First-class protected cruiser, 1882. Edgar class.
27. HMS *Wild Swan*: Sloop, 1876. Renamed *Columbine* in 1912.
28. HMS *Indefatigable*: Second-class cruiser, 1891. Apollo class.
29. HMS *Naiad*: Second-class cruiser, 1890. Apollo class.
30. HMS *Immortalité*: Armoured cruiser, 1887. Orlando class.
31. HMS *Undaunted*: Armoured cruiser, 1886. Orlando class.
32. HMS *Grafton*: Armoured cruiser, 1892. Edgar class.
33. HMS *Leander*: Cruiser, 1882. Sold in 1920.
34. HMS *Narcissus*: Belted cruiser, 1886. Apollo class.
35. RYS *Sunbeam*: Lord Brassey's famous auxiliary schooner, 532 tons, launched in 1874. He and his wife and family completed a world cruise of 37,000 miles in 1876–77. Lady Brassey's *A Voyage in the Sunbeam* was a bestseller.
36. HMS *Caledonia*: Wooden broadside ship launched in 1862. 6,830 tons, 12.5 knots, armament 7" B/L.
37. HMS *Brisk*: Cruiser, 1886. Sold in 1926.
38. HMS *Cossack*: Cruiser, 1886. Sold in 1905.
39. HMS *Brilliant*: Second-class cruiser, 1890. Apollo class.
40. HMS *Boxer*: Torpedo boat destroyer. W. S. L. was appointed lieutenant in command as of 18 August 1896. 'A' class, two-funnelled, 27 knots. Sunk in a 1918 collision.
41. HMS *Arethusa*: Second-class cruiser launched in 1882. Served in the Mediterranean Fleet, 1893–96.
42. HMS *Endymion*: Launched in 1891. Armoured cruiser. Edgar class.
43. HMS *Hood*: Battleship, Royal Sovereign class, launched 1891. 14,150 tons, 17.5 knots, armament 4×13.5", 10×6".
44. HMS *Jaseur*: Launched in 1892. Torpedo gunboat. Alarm class.
45. Simpson's: The bicycle would probably have been a Simpson cycle. The firm's London address was 119 Regent Street, W1. The chain referred to would certainly have been the Simpson 'Lever' chain, made by the Simpson Cycle Co., who claimed that it increased the power transmitted to the wheel. A leading cycle expert of the time described it as 'the greatest fraud ever foisted on the public'. One is a little surprised that W. S. L., with his sound practical naval training, should have fallen for the supposed merits of the 'Lever' chain. Alas, we do not know if he became disillusioned. The popularity of the device was deservedly short-lived, but a number of reputable cycle makers offered it as an optional extra fitting on certain of their machines.
46. HMS *Bruizer*: Torpedo-boat destroyer, commanded at the time by Lt Halsey, who became admiral. 'A' class destroyer. Speed 27 knots, two-funnelled.
47. HMS *Flora*: Second-class cruiser, 1893. Astraea class.

48. HMS *Theseus*: Second-class cruiser launched at Thames Iron Works in 1892. Edgar class.
49. HMS *Forte*: Second-class cruiser, 1893. Astraea class.
50. HMS *Revenge*: Battleship. Royal Sovereign class. Launched in 1892.
51. HMS *Dryad*: Launched in 1894. Torpedo gunboat, 1070 tons, 18.5 knots, armament 2×4.7", 4×3-pdr, 5×18" TT.
52. HMS *Barfleur*: Battleship launched in 1892. W. S. L. was appointed to her as of 20 January 1898. 10,500 tons, 18.5 knots, armament 4×10", 10×4.7", 7×18" TT.
53. HMS *Camperdown*: See HMS *Victoria*, note 20.
54. HMS *Scylla*: Second-class cruiser, 1891. Apollo class.
55. HMS *Tyne*: Destroyer depot and repair ship. Launched 1878. 3,560 tons, 11.7 knots, armament 1×12 pdr, 2×smw.
56. HMS *Ardent*: Torpedo-boat destroyer, launched in 1894.
57. HMS *Anson*: Battleship. Admiral class, launched in 1886. 10,600 tons, 17.2 knots, armament 4×13.5", 6×6".
58. HMS *Rodney*: Battleship. Admiral class, launched in 1884. 10,300 tons, 16.7 knots, armament 4×13.5", 6×6".
59. HMS *Dragon*: Destroyer, 'A' class. Four-funnelled, 27 knots. Launched in 1894.
60. HMS *Harrier*: Launched on 20 February 1894. Halcyon class twin-screw torpedo gunboat. 1,070 tons, 19 knots, armament 2×4.7", 4×6-pdrs, 5×18" TT. First commissioned for service in the Mediterranean on 14 January 1897. Sold in 1921.
61. HMS *Hibernia*: First-rater, launched in 1804. Became flagship of the Mediterranean Fleet Base, Malta, in 1855. Broken up in 1902.

List of Illustrations

(Dates in brackets refer to the relevant letters in the text.)

1. W. S. L. on the world voyage in *Wanderer RYS*.
2. The first of the quoted letters of W. S. L.
3. HMS *Britannia* and *Hindostan*. (10/2/1884, 30/11/1884, 1/2/1885, 29/9/1896)
4. Programme of concert given on HMS *Britannia*.
5. *Wanderer RYS*, from a painting by Admiral Richard Brydges Beechey. (25/4/1884, 1/7/1884, 14/7/1884)
6. *A Voyage round the World*, a painting by P. H. Calderon, RA.
7. W. S. L. at a tennis party at Ringlee, Queenstown.
8. The brigs HMS *Liberty* and HMS *Sealark*.
9. The Torpedo Class, Portsmouth, 1880. (4/5/1884, 5/1/1885, 1/2/1885)
10. Key to the above.
11. Officers of HMS *Triumph*.
12. HMS *Triumph* at Malta.
13. HMS *Triumph* at Esquimalt.
14. Admiral Sir Michael Culme-Seymour with his staff.
15. HMS *Triumph* off Cape de Gatte.
16. HMS *Orlando*. (14/9/1891)
17. HMS *Royalist*. (14/9/1891 et seq.)
18. HMS *Ringdove*. (14.9.1891)
19. Commander John Casement and officers of HMS *Rapid*. (15.5.1892)
20. HMS *Mercury*. (21.12.1892)
21. W. S. L.
22. Model of HMS *Alacrity*. (16/1/1893)
23. Model of HMS *Wivern*. (18/1/1893, 1/2/1893)
24. Officers of HMS *Caroline*. (19/2/1893)
25. HMS *Leander*. (11/1/1896)
26. Eclipse class protected cruiser.
27. HMS *Brilliant*. (15/7/1896 et seq.)
28. HMS *Endymion*. (25/7/1896)
29. HMS *Jaseur*. (31/7/1896)
30. The Simpson Road Racer. (10/8/1896)
31. The Simpson Lever Chain. (10/8/1986)

32. HM training brig *Martin*. (10/8/1896)
33. HMS *Boxer*. (25/7/1896 et seq.)
34. HMS *Bruizer*.
35. HMS *Flora*. (29/9/1896, 3/10/1896)
36. HMS *Bruizer*. (31/8/1896)
37. Officers of HMS *Bruizer*. (12/1/1897)
38. W. S. L. takes HMS *Boxer* out of Malta for Greece.
39. HMS *Ardent*. (9/3/1897)
40. HMS *Dragon*. (25/4/1897)
41. Officers of HMS *Boxer*.
42. HMS *Boxer*. The ship's company.
43. HMS *Barfleur*.
44. HMS *Duke of Wellington* and *Marlborough*.
45. W. S. L. in mufti.
46. W. S. L.'s wife Winnifred, née Hardy.
47. W. S. L. with his father-in-law, Mr Hardy.
48. W. S. L. in Scotland.
49. Winnifred Lambert in Scotland.
50. W. S. L. with his sister-in-law on the Thames.

Picture Credits

The Imperial War Museum (HMS *Ardent*, HMS *Barfleur*, HMS *Boxer*, HMS *Bruizer*, HMS *Dragon*, HMS *Endymion*, HMS *Flora*, HMS *Jaseur*, HMS *Mercury*, HMS *Orlando*, HMS *Ringdove*)

The Science Museum (HMS *Alacrity*, HMS *Wivern*)

Mrs Scott (Eclipse-class cruiser)

Rear-Admiral W. P. Mark-Wardlaw, RN (Mrs W. Lambert *c.* 1902)

All the remainders are from the original Lambert archives.

Acknowledgements

I am deeply indebted to the family of the late Reverend Prebendary R. G. Benson, QGM, who have so generously allowed me unrestricted access to the Lambert archives. I express my gratitude also to the family of Mrs Sally Fury for help in gathering other material connected with the Lambert family, of which she is herself a descendant.